The Way, the Truth & the Life Series

Teacher's Book 5

Key Stage 2

Sr. Marcellina Cooney, CP
Co-ordinating Editor

Religious Education series for 3 to 14 year olds

CATHOLIC TRUTH SOCIETY
PUBLISHERS TO THE HOLY SEE

Teacher's Book 5

Nihil obstat: Father Anton Cowan (Censor)
Imprimatur: The Rt Rev. Alan Hopes, VG, Auxiliary Bishop in Westminster, 25th March 2003, Feast of the Annunciation of the Lord.

The Nihil obstat *and* Imprimatur *are a declaration that the book or pamphlet is considered to be free from doctrinal or moral error. It is not implied that those who have granted the* Nihil obstat *and the* Imprimatur *agree with the contents, opinions or statements expressed.*

Design, compilation and format copyright © 2003 The Incorporated Catholic Truth Society.
Text copyright © 2003 Marcellina Cooney.
Published 2003 by The Incorporated Catholic Truth Society,
40-46 Harleyford Road, London SE11 5AY
Tel: 020 7640 0042 Fax: 020 7640 0046

ISBN: 978 1 86082 196 7 CTS Code: Pr 07
Designed and Produced by: The Catholic Truth Society.
Re-printed in the UK by: Thanet Press Ltd
Front Cover: The Resurrection © Peter Smith.

The following books are available from:
Redemptorists Publications, Chawton, Hampshire GU34 3HQ
Tel: 01420 88222; Fax: 01420 88805
Order Form: www.tere.org Publications Section

Primary
Syllabus for Key Stage 1
Foundation Stage CD ROM (age 3-5) [see www.tere.org Publications]
Book 1 Big Book, Pupil's Workbook and Teacher's Book (Year 1, age 5-6)
Book 2 Pupil's and Teacher's Books (age 6-7)
Syllabus for Key Stage 2
Book 3 Pupil's and Teacher's Books (Year 3, age 7-8)
Book 4 Pupil's and Teacher's Books (Year 4, age 8-9)
Book 5 Pupil's and Teacher's Books (Year 5, age 9-10)
Book 6 Pupil's and Teacher's Books (Year 7, age 10-11)

Secondary
The Way, Student's and Teacher's Books (Year 7, age 11-12)
The Truth, Student's and Teacher's Books (Year 8, age 12-13)
The Life, Student's and Teacher's Books (Year 9, age 13-14)

Supplementary resources for Teachers, Parents and Pupils can be found on the website www.tere.org developed to support this series.

Teacher's Book 5

INTRODUCTION

The teaching of Religious Education to young children is very challenging. It is particularly difficult to convey theological concepts in a stimulating and meaningful way. Consequently, teachers of these age groups need the help and support of good teaching resources in Religious Education.

I am very pleased to welcome and introduce this Teacher's Book, which forms part of the Key Stage 2 material - *The Way, the Truth and the Life series* - being published by the CTS.

The Syllabus, Pupil's and Teacher's Books, which make up this series are based on the *Religious Education Curriculum Directory* for Catholic Schools published by the Bishops' Conference in 1996. The Curriculum directory is based on the content of the *Catechism of the Catholic Church*.

This project is the fruit of hard work and co-operation between a number of teachers across the country. I thank them, and their collaborators, for all their effort.

Monsignor Michael Keegan has been a great source of encouragement to the teachers involved and produced the theological notes for each of the modules in the syllabus. I thank him warmly.

I trust that all who use this Teacher's Book 5 and the corresponding Pupil's Book 5 will find them a direct, clear help in the important tasks of enabling their pupils to learn about the Catholic faith and to respond to its invitation with growing faith and generosity.

✢ Vincent Nichols
Archbishop of Birmingham

Teacher's Book 5

NOTE FOR USERS

The contents of this **Teacher's Book** and the companion **Pupil's Book 5** are based on the **Key Stage 2 Syllabus**, which is published as a separate document in this series. These resources cover all the essential content of the *Religious Education Curriculum Directory* of the Bishops' Conference of England and Wales (RECD).

The **Syllabus** incorporates two attainment targets: learning *about* the Catholic faith (AT1) and learning *from* Catholic faith (AT2). These are set out in the form of specific key learning objectives for each module, and listed at the start of each section in both Teacher and Pupil's Books. This syllabus can be used as a guide in curriculum planning or as a framework for developing a scheme of work.

In the **Teacher's Book**, the key learning objectives are further developed for each module in the form of a **Theological Introduction** to enrich the teacher's understanding of the content they are about to teach. They are based mainly on the *Catechism of the Catholic Church* (CCC). The **starting points, additional activities, additional resources** and **photocopyable worksheets** are all intended to complement the Pupil's Book and provide suggestions for differentiated work. The inclusion of website addresses does not necessarily mean that everything on them would be appropriate and therefore should be used at the teacher's discretion.

The section on **assessment** offers some guidance on different ways of monitoring pupils' progress. The **Level Descriptors** are based on the non-statutory guidance on RE produced by the Qualifications and Curriculum Authority. These descriptors have been modified so that they apply specifically to the content of the syllabus and Pupil's Book 5. The exemplar **assessment tasks** based on each module or unit of work are intended as guidance for teachers.

Teachers will want to enrich further the variety of resources with the use of videos, audio CDs, websites and the use of ICT in general. It is our intention to update our website *www.tere.org* regularly with additional resources for teachers, parents and pupils, so that the content of what is being taught in the classroom is readily accessible to all. We welcome contributions from schools. These should be sent to CTS for the attention of the co-ordinating editor of this book.

ACKNOWLEDGMENTS

Very grateful thanks are expressed to all those who collaborated in preparing this Teacher's Book, in particular:

Farleigh School, Andover; Our Lady of Lourdes School, Barnet; Sacred Heart School, Barnet; St Vincent's School, Barnet; St Teresa's School, Harrow; Notre Dame School, Greenwich; Presentation College, Reading.

Theological Introductions to the Modules: Mgr Michael Keegan.

Editorial Team: Louise McKenna, Amette Ley, Elizabeth Redmond, Anthony O'Rourke, Laura Lamb, Clare Watkins and Marcellina Cooney.

Professional Curriculum Adviser: Margaret Cooling.

Illustration: *'Prayer Symbol'*, p.78, by Andras Simon, Hungary.

Poems: *'De-Creators'*, p.54, by Sr Leo OSC. *'Adam'*, p.56, by G Rust from *Breaking the Chains*, © Nelson Word. *'The World'*, p.58, by W Brighty Rands, from *Whispering in God's Ear*, collated by Alan MacDonald, Lion, 1994. *'A Thinking Christmas'*, p.61, by Wes Magee.

(For those images and poems for which we have been unable to trace the copyright holder, the Publisher would be grateful to receive any information.)

CONTENTS

Introduction 3
Note for Users 4
Acknowledgments 4
Overview of Syllabus - Key Stage 2 6
Methodology 7

1. Gifts From God 8
Key Learning Objectives 8
Theological Introduction 9
Points for Discussion and Further Activities 11

2. The Commandments 15
Key Learning Objectives 15
Theological Introduction 16
Points for Discussion and Further Activities 17

3. Inspirational People 22
Key Learning Objectives 22
Theological Introduction 23
Points for Discussion and Further Activities 24

4. Reconciliation 29
Key Learning Objectives 29
Theological Introduction 30
Points for Discussion and Further Activities 32

5. Life in the Risen Jesus 37
Key Learning Objectives 37
Theological Introduction 38
Points for Discussion and Further Activities 40

6. People of Other Faiths 45
Key Learning Objectives 45
Theological Introduction 46
Points for Discussion and Further Activities 48

Photocopy Worksheets 51

Assessment and Levels of Achievement 86
Introduction 86
Levels of Achievement 87

Assessment Tasks 89
Guidance on Marking Assessment Tasks 95

OVERVIEW OF KEY STAGE 2 SYLLABUS

	Autumn 1	Autumn 2	Spring 1	Spring 2	Summer 1	Summer 2
YEAR 3	3.1 The Christian Family	3.2 Mary, Our Mother	3.3 Called to Change	3.4 Eucharist	3.5 Celebrating Easter & Pentecost	3.6 Being a Christian
YEAR 4	4.1 The Bible	4.2 Trust in God	4.3 Jesus, the Teacher	4.4 Jesus, the Saviour	4.5 Mission of the Church	4.6 Belonging to the Church
YEAR 5	5.1 Gifts from God	5.2 The Commandments	5.3 Inspirational People	5.4 Reconciliation	5.5 Life in the Risen Jesus	5.6 People of Other Faiths
YEAR 6	6.1 The Kingdom of God	6.2 Justice	6.3 Jesus, Son of God	6.4 Jesus, the Bread of Life	6.5 The Work of the Apostles	6.6 Called to Serve

METHODOLOGY

Our primary focus in presenting the religious content specified by the *Religious Education Curriculum Directory* [RECD] should be REVELATION. God is always the initiator in the history of our creation and redemption; it is his revealing of himself that makes classroom religious education possible.

However, it is essential that we set the scene by giving an overall picture of what we are going to study: if it is Creation we should have pictures of nature and some environmental issues or if it is the Ten Commandments maybe headlines from newspapers so that pupils will be able to make the connection between belief and behaviour. We should try to relate religious content to life around us and make connections with what has gone before so that they will be able to see the relevance of what they are studying.

It is proposed that each of the following areas should, as far as possible, be covered in each Book of the Primary and Secondary series.

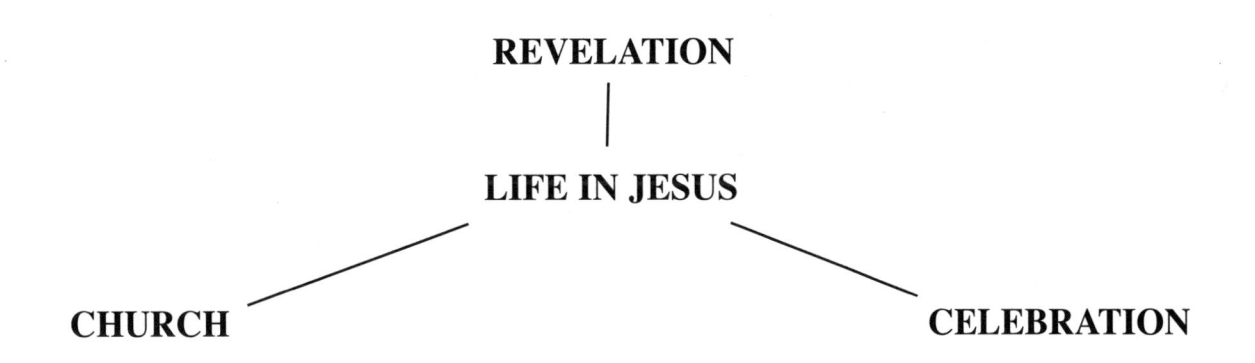

```
              REVELATION
                  |
              LIFE IN JESUS
             /            \
       CHURCH          CELEBRATION
```

Attempts to make clear connections between the truths of faith and the pupils' own experiences of life are essential. For many, it is only when they see the relevance to their own lives of what they are learning that they become fully engaged in it. At times, this will mean starting with the pupils' experience. For example, in studying 'conflict and reconciliation' we might well want to begin with reflection on conflict in the lives and experiences of the pupils. Nevertheless, REVELATION, in the strict sense of the word, would remain the starting point for the delivery and presentation of the specifically religious content material. We would look, in other words, at conflict in our world and in our lives as a sort of background, and then begin our **religious** education proper with how Christian Revelation addresses itself to conflict in human life.

"The Gospel message always, at some point, takes the person beyond the scope of their own experience, challenging and transforming it. It is a message of a saving and transforming gift."
(Archbishop Vincent Nichols)

1 GIFTS FROM GOD

"Creation is the first and universal revelation of God's love. As the action of Father, Son and Holy Spirit, creation is the first step towards the covenant relationship God seeks with every human being. Each person is created in the image of God and called by grace to this covenant relationship." (RECD p.14)

"Each human person is unique and made in God's image and likeness, having the rights of a person from the moment of conception... Love of neighbour is expressed in respect for life at all stages, especially the life of those who cannot defend themselves, including the yet unborn. Respect for and development of human life requires us to work for justice in society and peace between peoples and nations." (RECD p.34-35)

Key learning objectives:

AT 1
In this unit you will have the opportunity to:

- know the story of Creation and the Fall in Genesis;

- understand that we are all created in the image and likeness of God;

- know that God calls us to care for each other and all creation with love and respect;

- know that there are times when we fail to be good stewards of creation;

- know about people who show great respect for the weakest members of society;

- know about people who show great respect for creation.

AT 2
You will have the chance to:

- appreciate how we can show respect for ourselves, for others and for God;

- reflect on times we have failed to show respect;

- reflect on the gifts and talents God has given each of us;

- reflect on the use/misuse we can make of these gifts.

THEOLOGICAL INTRODUCTION

Q. What does the first chapter of Genesis teach us?

"God himself created the visible world in all its richness, diversity and order. Scripture presents the work of the Creator symbolically as a succession of six days of divine 'work', concluded by the 'rest' of the seventh day..." (*CCC 337*).

"*Nothing exists that does not owe its existence to God the Creator.* The world began when God's word drew it out of nothingness; all existent beings, all of nature, and all human history are rooted in this primordial event, the very genesis by which the world was constituted and time began." (*CCC 338*).

"*Each creature possesses its own particular goodness and perfection.* For each one of the works of the 'six days' it is said: 'And God saw that it was good.' By the very nature of creation, material being is endowed with its own stability, truth and excellence, its own order and laws. Each of the various creatures, willed in its own being, reflects in its own way a ray of God's infinite wisdom and goodness. Man must therefore respect the particular goodness of every creature, to avoid any disordered use of things which would be in contempt of the Creator and would bring disastrous consequences for human beings and their environment." (*CCC 339*).

"God wills the *interdependence of creatures*. The sun and the moon, the cedar and the little flower, the eagle and the sparrow: the spectacle of their countless diversities and inequalities tells us that no creature is self-sufficient. Creatures exist only in dependence on each other, to complete each other, in the service of each other." (*CCC 340, see also 341 - 349*).

Q. What does it mean to say we are made in the image and likeness of God?

"*Man is the summit* of the Creator's work, as the inspired account expresses by clearly distinguishing the creation of man from that of the other creatures." (*CCC 343*).

"'God created man in his own image, in the image of God he created him, male and female he created them.' Man occupies a unique place in creation: (I) he is 'in the image of God'; (II) in his own nature he unites the spiritual and material worlds; (III) he is created 'male and female'; (IV) God established him in his friendship." (*CCC 355*).

"Of all visible creatures only man is 'able to know and love his creator'. He is 'the only creature on earth that God has willed for its own sake', he alone is called to share, by knowledge and love, in God's own life..." (*CCC 356*). "Being in the image of God the human individual possesses the dignity of a *person*, ...he is called by grace to a covenant with his Creator, to offer him a response of faith and love that no other creature can give in his stead." (*CCC 357*).

"God created everything for man, but man in turn was created to serve and love God and to offer all creation back to him..." (*CCC 358*).

Gifts from God

Q. What does it mean to have a body and soul?

"In Sacred Scripture the term '*soul*' often refers to human *life* or the entire human *person*. But 'soul' also refers to the innermost aspect of man, that which is of greatest value in him, that by which he is most especially in God's image: 'soul' signifies the s*piritual principle* in man." (*CCC 363*).

"The human *body* shares in the dignity of the 'image of God': it is human body precisely because it is animated by a human soul, and it is the whole human person that is intended to become, in the body of Christ, a temple of the Spirit:

> Man, though made of body and soul, is a unity. Through his very bodily condition he sums up in himself the elements of the material world. Through him they are thus brought to their highest perfection and can raise their voice in praise freely given to the Creator. For this reason a man may not despise his bodily life. Rather he is obliged to regard his body as good and to hold it in honour since God has created it and will raise it up on the last day." (*CCC 364*).

Q. What is the meaning of the 'Fall' in Genesis?

"Freedom put to the test: God created man in his image and established him in his friendship. A spiritual creature, man can live this friendship only in free submission to God. The prohibition against eating 'of the tree of the knowledge of good and evil' spells this out: 'for in the day that you eat of it, you shall die.' (*Gen 2:17*) The 'tree of the knowledge of good and evil' symbolically evokes the insurmountable limits that man, being a creature, must freely recognise and respect with trust. Man is dependent on his Creator, and subject to the laws of creation and to the moral norms that govern the use of freedom." (*CCC 396*).

Q. What is Original Sin?

"Man, tempted by the devil, let his trust in his Creator die in his heart and, abusing his freedom, *disobeyed* God's command. This is what man's first sin consisted of. All subsequent sin would be disobedience toward God and lack of trust in his goodness." (*CCC 397*).

"Scripture portrays the tragic consequences of the first disobedience. Adam and Eve immediately lose the grace of original holiness..." (*CCC 399*) "The harmony in which they had found themselves, thanks to original justice, is now destroyed..." (*CCC 400*).

Q. What are the consequences of Adam's sin for us?

"All men are implicated in Adam's sin, as St Paul affirms: 'By one man's disobedience many (that is, all men) were made sinners': 'sin came into the world through one man and death through sin, and so death spread to all men because all men sinned...' (*CCC 403*).

Q. How did the sin of Adam become the sin of all his descendants?

"...The transmission of original sin is a mystery that we cannot fully understand. But we do know by Revelation that Adam had received original holiness and justice not for himself alone, but for all human nature. By yielding to the tempter, Adam and Eve committed a *personal sin*, but this sin affected the *human nature* that they would then transmit *in a fallen state*. It is a sin which will be transmitted by propagation to all mankind, that is, by the transmission of a human nature deprived of original holiness and justice. And

Gifts from God

that is why original sin is called 'sin' only in an analogical sense: it is a sin 'contracted' and not 'committed' - a state and not an act. (*CCC 404*).

Q. How should we use the gift of creation?
"The seventh commandment enjoins respect for the integrity of creation. Animals, like plants and inanimate beings, are by nature designed for the common good of past, present and future humanity. Use of the minerals, vegetable and animal resources of the universe cannot be divorced from moral imperatives. Man's dominion over inanimate and other living beings granted by the Creator is not absolute; it is limited by concern for the quality of life of his neighbour, including generations to come, it requires a religious respect for the integrity of creation." (*CCC 2415*). "*Animals* are God's creatures... We should recall the gentleness with which saints like St Francis of Assisi and St Philip Neri treated animals." (*CCC 2416*).

"God entrusted animals to the stewardship of those whom he had created in his own image. Hence it is legitimate to use animals for food and clothing. They may be domesticated to help man in his work and leisure. Medical and scientific experimentation on animals is morally acceptable practice if it remains in reasonable limits and contributes to caring for or saving human lives." (*CCC 2417*).

"It is contrary to human dignity to cause animals to suffer or die needlessly. It is likewise unworthy to spend money on them that should as a priority go to the relief of human misery. One can love animals; one should not direct to them the affection due only to persons." (*CCC 2418*). "There is a *solidarity among all creatures* arising from the fact that all have the same Creator and are all ordered to his glory:.." (*CCC 344*).

Q. Does our scientific knowledge of Creation conflict with the account in Genesis?
Science and religion are not rivals - they each deal with different aspects of reality. Religion adds to our scientific understanding by adding an extra essential dimension. The fact that **God** created the universe is basic Catholic doctrine. But **how God did it** is not revealed in the Bible, that is the work of scientific discovery.

POINTS FOR DISCUSSION AND FURTHER ACTIVITIES

LEARNING OBJECTIVE: know the story of Creation in Genesis and think about its meaning

Starting points
Start by looking at some aspect of nature, a plant, flowers, clouds in the sky or birds in the air. Help pupils to observe some aspect in detail. If possible take pupils out to a park or a garden to help them reflect on the wonder of nature; encourage them to focus on one particular thing and examine it very closely.

Develop thinking skills:
- Think of something about nature that amazes you.
- What does it tell you about its maker?
- Has it come into existence just by chance?
- Why do you think God gave us such a variety of flowers, trees, birds, fish, animals etc.? List some of them to show the abundance of gifts we have been given.

Gifts from God

- What are the gifts God has given to you? (*Eyes, ears, hands, gift of speech, hearing, vision, ability to walk, sing, dance, etc.*)
- How can we use these gifts to help others?

Additional Activities:
- Watch the beginning of the BBC video Pathways of Belief 'Christianity' for images of creation and children explaining what God made.
- Invite the pupils to use their senses to describe their four favourite things from creation - what they like to smell, look at, eat, etc. and to give a reason for their choice.
- Another way of doing activity 4 page 5 would be to place a chair in the middle of the room or a hula-hoop. Play soft music and invite pupils to write down questions that they would like to ask God about Creation. Then pick up a question and with the pupils discuss how God might answer it.
- Watch section of video 'Living it Out' part 1 where pupils talk about using their gifts and how Carla, an artist, uses her gifts. It goes on to tell the story of Creation from Genesis.
- Make up a prayer to thank God for all his gifts using pictures and words and choose some music to go with it so that it could be used for a morning assembly.

LEARNING OBJECTIVE: know that God calls us to care for Creation

Starting points

Watch the clip of the video 'Living it Out' where the pupils in a school talk about what they are doing to save the environment. Use this video to lead into a discussion of what your school can do to protect the school environment. This could lead to a discussion on the local environment. Is there anyone the pupils can write to in order to make suggestions on how to improve the environment for young children, elderly people and those with disabilities?

An alternative would be to look at the video Pathways of Belief: 'Christianity' for similar ideas of how to protect the environment and to be good stewards of the earth.

Additional Activities:
- Think of ways in which you can share your gifts...
    I can show my care for the world by ....
    I can show my care for people by ....
    I can show my care for animals by ....
- Worksheet 'Humans / Animals' page 53 This should give pupils the opportunity to reflect on the fact that we are both physical and spiritual.
- Worksheet 'Stewards of the Earth' page 52. This worksheet will provide opportunities for pupils to reflect on how they can take care of their environment and make links with Citizenship.
- Worksheet 'De-Creators page 54.
- Worksheet writing frame 'A Persuasive Letter!' page 55. This is to help pupils develop their literacy skills in writing a persuasive letter. Encourage them to think carefully about what would persuade them to change their behaviour.
- A poem De-Creators Pupil's Book page 10, which could be used for 'Collective Worship'

Gifts from God

- Try the BBC's 'Gardening with Children' website which offers projects for home and school. For example 'Home-grown projects: Choose from one of 24 projects; whatever the weather, there's always something to do' *www.bbc.co.uk/gardening/children*

LEARNING OBJECTIVE: know and reflect on the story of the Fall

Starting points
We believe that God gave all people freedom to choose between **right and wrong**. Christians differ over the story of Adam and Eve: some see it as a story with a theological truth and some see it as history. We believe that this story helps us to understand things about our lives today. We know that the world is not as God intended it to be:

Invite pupils to explore human situations of good and evil, kindness and selfishness etc. Provide an opportunity for them to reflect on the **choices** we make and the **consequences** of our actions. Choose classroom situations e.g. - if the pupils are left alone for a few minutes what is likely to happen; if the teacher is occupied writing something on the board, does everyone continue working as if he/she was being watched?

In groups invite pupils to recall a decision they have made, what happened as a result of that decision and how they felt about it. Would they do anything now to change that decision?

Additional Activities:
- Worksheet 'Who's fault was it?' page 57.
- Worksheet on poem 'Adam' by G Rust page 56.

LEARNING OBJECTIVE: know about individuals who inspire us to respect creation and look after the vulnerable members of society

Additional story about St Francis
One day Francis left his companions who were walking with him along a path and dashed eagerly into the field. 'Peace be with you!' he called out to the rooks and pigeons, starlings and crows, and, instead of rising and flying away they stood waiting for him. He was thrilled and began talking to them just as if they were people.
'My brother birds,' he said, 'your Creator has given you feathers for clothing, wings for flying and the wide sky for your home. You are the luckiest creatures in the world and should love God and thank him for his kindness.' While Frances talked the birds stretched out their necks towards him, spread their wings and opened their beaks as if they understood every word. He blessed them and then gave each one of them permission to fly away. Off they went North, South, East and West forming a huge cross in the sky.

Additional resource:
Use the video 'St Francis and his Friends' to show the following episodes in different lessons:
- Francis taming the wolf of Gubbio;
- Francis preaching to the birds;
- Francis healing a man with leprosy.

Gifts from God

Collective Worship

Use the 'Canticle of St Francis' page 59 pupils could add to it by selecting an appropriate hymn and closing prayer.

Additional Resources

Video 'Living it Out' Christianity in Everyday Life, Grayswood Production Ltd., Willow Grange, Woking Road, Guilford, Surrey GU4 7PZ (Tel. 01483 578967)
Video BBC Pathways of Belief: Christianity, Programme 1 Creation
Video BBC Pathways of Belief: Judaism, Programme 1 God
Video St Francis & His Friends, Pauline Books & Media

Cafod, 2 Romero Close, Stockwell, London SW9 9TY
Christian Aid, PO BOX 100, London SE1 7RT
Tear Fund, 100 Church Road, Teddington, Middlesex TW11 8PY
Christian Ecology Link, 20 Carlton Road, Harrogate, North Yorkshire HG2 8DD

2 THE COMMANDMENTS

"The Ten Commandments are the word of God, regarded in the Old Testament as a gift and sign of God's love. They express the implications of belonging to God through the covenant of Sinai. Jesus summed them up saying, "This is the first and greatest commandment: You shall love the Lord your God with all your heart, and with all your soul, and with all your mind. The second is this: You shall love your neighbour as yourself." (RECD p.35)

Key learning objectives:

AT 1
In this unit you will have the opportunity to:

- know that God loves us and calls us into relationship with him;

- know that God gave Moses the Ten Commandments on Mount Sinai because he loves us;

- understand that the Ten Commandments are a gift from God to help us;

- know how Jesus summarised the Ten Commandments (*Mt* 22:36-40);

- understand how we can show our love for God by keeping his commandments;

- know that God sent his Son Jesus into the world because he loves us.

AT 2
You will have the the chance to:

- appreciate how God has shown his love for us;

- reflect on ways we can deepen our relationship with God;

- reflect on how the birth of Jesus at Christmas is a sign of God's love for us.

The Commandments

THEOLOGICAL INTRODUCTION

Q. Where did the Ten Commandments come from?

"The word 'Decalogue' means literally 'ten words'. God revealed these 'ten words' to his people on the holy mountain. They were written 'with the finger of God', unlike the other commandments written by Moses. They are pre-eminently the words of God. They are handed on to us in the books of *Exodus* and *Deuteronomy*... It is in the New Covenant in Jesus Christ that their full meaning will be revealed." (*CCC 2056*).

"The 'ten words'... belong to God's revelation of himself and his glory. The gift of the Commandments is the gift of God himself and his holy will. In making his will known, God reveals himself to his people." (*CCC 2059*).
"The gift of the Commandments and of the Law is part of the covenant God sealed with his own. In *Exodus*, the revelation of the 'ten words' is granted between the proposal of the covenant and its conclusion - after the people had committed themselves to 'do' all that the Lord had said and to 'obey' it. The Decalogue is never handed on without first recalling the covenant ('The Lord our God made a covenant with us in Horeb')." (*CCC 2060*).

Q. What was the context of the Ten Commandments?
Q. What is their purpose?

"The Commandments take on their full meaning within the covenant. According to Scripture, man's moral life has all its meaning in and through the covenant. The first of the 'ten words' recalls that God loved his people first:... 'I am the Lord your God, who brought you out of the land of Egypt, out of the house of slavery.'" (*CCC 2061*).

"The Commandments properly so-called come in the second place: they express the implications of belonging to God through the establishment of the covenant. Moral existence is a *response* to the Lord's loving initiative. It is the acknowledgement and homage given to God and a worship of thanksgiving. It is co-operation with the plan God pursues in history." (*CCC 2062*). "The Ten Commandments state what is required in the love of God and love of neighbour..." (*CCC 2067*). "...Man's vocation is to make God manifest by acting in conformity with his creation 'in the image and likeness of God:..'" (*CCC 2085*).

Q. What does Jesus say about the Ten Commandments?
Q. What do they teach us?

"'Teacher, what good must I do, to have eternal life?' To the young man who asked this question, Jesus answers first by invoking the necessity to recognise God as the 'One there is who is good', as the supreme Good and the source of all good. Then Jesus tells him: 'If you would enter into life, keep the commandments.'..." (*CCC 2052*).

"The Ten Commandments belong to God's revelation. At the same time they teach us the true humanity of man. They bring to light the essential duties, and therefore, indirectly, the fundamental rights inherent in the nature of the human person..." (*CCC 2070*).

Q. How did Jesus summarise the Ten Commandments?

"When someone asks him, 'Which commandment in the Law is the greatest?' Jesus replies: 'You shall love the Lord your God with all your heart, and with all your soul, and with all your mind. This is the greatest

The Commandments

and the first commandment. And a second is like it: You shall love your neighbour as yourself. On these two commandments hang all the Law and the prophets.'..." (*CCC 2055*).

Q. What help does Jesus give us to keep the Commandments?
"Jesus says: 'I am the vine, you are the branches. He who abides in me, and I in him, he it is that bears much fruit, for apart from me you can do nothing.' The fruit referred to in this saying is the holiness of life made fruitful by union with Christ. When we believe in Jesus Christ, partake of his mysteries and keep his commandments, the Saviour himself comes to love, in us, his Father and his brethren, our Father and our brethren. His person becomes, through the Spirit, the living and interior rule of our activity. 'This is my commandment, that you love one another as I have loved you.'" (*CCC 2074*).

Q. Why was Jesus sent into the world?
"But when the time had fully come, God sent forth his Son, born of a woman, born under the law, to redeem those who were under the law, so that we might receive adoption as sons.' This is 'the gospel of Jesus Christ, the Son of God': God has visited his people. He has fulfilled the promise he made to Abraham and his descendants. He acted far beyond all expectation - he has sent his own 'beloved Son'." (*CCC 422*). "...'*For us men and for our salvation* he came down from heaven;'..." (*CCC 456*).

SUMMARY

The New Covenant is a gift of God by which he chooses us to be his people and enables us to live lives which are a share in the divine life. This began at Sinai when God chose the Israelites to be his own people. They, in their turn, agreed to do all that the Lord commanded. God's will was made manifest in the gift of the Ten Commandments, which teach us how to live holy lives. The Law taught what to do but did not contain the means for fulfilling the Law. Only in the New Covenant, through our Lord Jesus Christ, are we enabled to keep the commandments. The Old Covenant prepared the way for the revelation of the New Covenant. Jesus deepened the meaning of the Ten Commandments and gave us a new motivation for keeping them. We are to love one another as he has loved us. By the gift of the Holy Spirit we are enabled to live in Jesus and according to his word. He teaches us to live holy lives in this world and so come to the reward of eternal life in heaven.

POINTS FOR DISCUSSION AND FURTHER ACTIVITIES

LEARNING OBJECTIVE: **know that God gave the Ten Commandments to Moses**

Starting points
Recap briefly on how Moses led the people out of Egypt - see story of Moses & the Exodus in WTL Teacher's Book 4 pages 44 - 46. The aim now is to build on pupils' prior knowledge of Moses.

When God gave the Ten Commandments to Moses he wanted to guide them into ways of living a good life - a life that would be good for them. God was making a **covenant** with them, that is, a very solemn promise, that he would be their God and they would be his people. The Hebrew people (Jews) had to promise that they would worship God alone and in return God would always look after them. "I will be your God and you will be my people". (Exodus 6:7)

The Commandments

Additional Activities:
- Take time to **reflect** with pupils on why we need rules.
- What would our school be like if there were no rules?
- Imagine what it would be like if there was no highway code - what would the traffic be like?
- Are there rules at home? Why?
- Do rules help to make life easier or more difficult?
- Brainstorm all the advantages of having rules - show respect, concern for others, teach us how to live a good life, etc
- Show the last 15 minutes of the video 'The Ten Commandments' Cecil B. DeMille's (with Charlton Heston as Moses).

LEARNING OBJECTIVE: understand that the Ten Commandments are a gift from God to help us

Starting points

In this section it is important to keep interest alive, rather like a soap opera, imagine what the outcome will be. It may not be possible to do all the activities or it may be necessary to put two RE lessons together.

Sometimes it will help to use an overhead projector to discuss the pros and cons of the new versions of the Commandments. This could also be done by getting the whole class to focus on the problems that arise and the reasons for them, so sometimes it will be predicting what will happen next.

Create a safe environment where pupils can express their beliefs without fear of being put-down by others. Make sure pupils are aware of why it is important for them to know about the Ten Commandments today.

Discuss the purpose of rules. Invite pupils to think about whether knowing the purpose help us to keep them. Note that when doing the activities on page 25 there are likely to be pupils in the class who do not see any harm in shoplifting.

Be aware that the activities in the Pupil's Book provide opportunities for developing a variety of skills, for example:

- Analysing - what the Commandment actually means.
- Deducing - if X is true, then it means that people should...
- Evaluating - do I agree with it or is it important?
- Applying - how do I or other people live this Commandment today?
- Predicting - do you think this version will work? Why, why not?
- Problem solving - what to do to put things right again.

The pupils with logical/mathematical minds will enjoy solving the problems and coming up with solutions. The kinaesthetic type will enjoy role-playing.

The Commandments

Additional Activities:
- Use role-play and ask the pupils to enact one of the Commandments being broken and then discuss the implications of it: what effect does it have on the individual(s), their family, friends, school etc. How will that person feel later on that evening when he/she reflects on his/her behaviour?
- Use examples of the Commandments being kept or broken in daily life from magazines, newspapers, the news on TV etc. Look at the consequences of what happens so that pupils will form the habit of reflecting on their own behaviour. Seek opportunities to highlight good deeds and how this helps to make people build up a positive self-image.
- Stop teaching and give the pupils five minutes to sum up what they have learned so far or give them five minutes to memorise what they have learned and then to share it with the person next to them.
- Make a list of ten rules that you have to follow (at home, in school and elsewhere) e.g
   Don't drop litter in the streets
   Go to bed on time
   Pay attention in lessons
- In a table, list which of these rules you find easy to follow and which you find difficult.
- If you were in charge of your own rules, would you change any of them? Why or why not?
- Write about a time in your life when it was hard to do the right thing.
- Choose one of the 'Headlines' in the Pupil's Book and explain what you think are the reasons for it.
- Imagine you are a journalist. Pick one of the 'Headline Stories' and write what the rest of the report said.
- "Prisons are emptying survey shows". Can you explain why the prisons would be emptying under New Rules Version 2?
- Why do you think the New Rules Version 3 have not been a success?

LEARNING OBJECTIVE: reflect on the birth of Jesus

Starting points

It is important to spend some time reflecting on the fact that we need God's help in order to be able to keep the Commandments. Then lead on to the account of how God sent his only Son Jesus into the world to show us how to live and give us the help we need.

Reflect on how Jesus, who is truly God and truly human, came down to earth as a tiny baby. He had to go to school and learn how to read and write. Just imagine if our Head Teacher had to start again in Year 1 what would she/he find most difficult. Arrange for the pupils to interview the Head and use this as a way of introducing the idea of Jesus coming to earth for us.

This is the time now to prepare for the birth of Jesus; to be aware of how much we need his help and to spend time inviting him to come into our hearts in a new way this Christmas.

Additional Activities:
- Spend some time unpacking the meaning of the word INCARNATION; it is about Jesus giving up his power and becoming one of us. He became one of us. He experiences life's 'ups and downs', just as we do. He knew what it was like to be sad, happy, etc. therefore when we speak to him he knows how we feel.

The Commandments

- Choose a Christmas Carol.
- Use the worksheet 'Christmas' page 61 and invite pupils to write their own poem 'A Joyful Christmas' - encourage them to think of what brings true happiness in life. Reflect back on the Commandments and think of who should come first in our lives. Is going to Mass an important event that will give them true peace? Think of some of the ways they could help at home. What little surprise could they plan to make life easier for their mother?
- For Collective Worship see 'Blessing the Christmas Crib' and 'Blessing the Christmas Tree' on *www.tere.org* section for Primary Schools 'Collective Worship'.

ICT

www.ainglkiss.com/10com/ An explanation of each of the Commandments.
www.cptryon.org/prayer/child/adv.html Advent wreath & prayers for each week.

Video

Video 'The Ten Commandments' Cecil B. DeMille's CTS or St Paul's Multimedia.

Guided Meditation on the Birth of Jesus

It is a cold chilly night when we come across shepherds looking after their sheep on a hillside. They huddle around a fire and invite us to join them. We are all feeling drowsy and close to falling asleep, then, suddenly there is a very bright light. I thought it was lightning or maybe a ghost. Now we see a beautiful angel in the sky, coming towards us. He says:

"Do not be afraid. Listen, I bring you news of great joy, a joy to be shared by the whole people. Today in the town of David a saviour has been born to you: He is Christ the Lord. And here is a sign for you: you will find a baby wrapped in swaddling clothes and lying in a manger." And suddenly with the angel there were many others praising God and singing:

*'Glory to God in the highest heaven,
and peace among people with whom he is pleased'.*

The angels vanish. We sit in silence looking at each other. Then one of the shepherds jumps up and says, "lets go and find out if it is true". The shepherds know the way so we keep close to them. They seem to be following a star, they avoid the hotels and make their way towards stables for animals - I remember the angel said you will find him lying in a manger!

"I bet that is the place", one of them shouts, pointing to a cave with a star shining over it. We creep in quietly behind the shepherds. There she is, a young woman holding a newborn baby. It is Mary with the baby Jesus and Joseph is keeping a close eye on them.

This is a very precious moment. I thank God for sending Jesus to us. I tell Jesus that I want to love him and stay very close to him. We all take a few minutes to tell him our own private thoughts and ask for his help.

It is now time for us to leave. As we make our way home we sing: "Away in a Manger".

Inspirational People

3 INSPIRATIONAL PEOPLE

"Love of neighbour involves respect for the integrity of all creation. It involves working for a just society, both locally and internationally, so that all are assured of fair access to the means of life and work. It includes love for the poor, which results in the practical aid of our neighbours in their spiritual and bodily needs.

Love of neighbour is also an expression of our search for God. This love leads to a 'purity of heart' and integrity which 'hunger and thirst for justice'. This love and integrity inform all our attitudes to possessions and wealth." (RECD p.35)

Key learning objectives:

AT 1
In this unit you will have the opportunity to:

- know the conditions for following Jesus; [*Mk* 12:29-30; *Matt* 18:22; *Lk* 9:23-26]

- know how Jesus described a true disciple; [*Lk* 6:27-38 & 46-49; *Matt* 25:35-40]

- know that in order to gain eternal life we have to respond to the graces God has given to us;

- know the story of a person who showed great love for others, e.g. Bakhita;

- know the story of a person who had a special love for those rejected by society, e.g. Damien;

- know the story of a person who was an inspiration for young people e.g. Dominic Savio, Maria Goretti;

- identify people today who are an inspiration in their service of others.

AT 2
You will have the chance to:

- take time to reflect on our commitment to following Jesus;

- reflect on how we can serve others at home, school, locally, globally;

- know that Lent is a time when we can make small sacrifices to show our love for God and for others.

THEOLOGICAL INTRODUCTION

Q. What are the conditions for following Jesus

According to Mark's Gospel, 12:29-30, the love of God with all our heart, with all our soul, with all our mind and with all our strength is a characteristic of true followers of Jesus. St Matthew, 18:12, adds that they should be willing to forgive unconditionally, and St Luke, 9:23-26, records how Jesus said, 'If anyone wants to be a true follower of mine, let him renounce himself and take up his cross everyday and follow me. For anyone who wants to save his life will lose it; but anyone who loses his life for my sake, that man will save it. What gain, then, is it for a man to have won the whole world and to have lost or ruined his very self? For if anyone is ashamed of me and of my words, of him the Son of man will be ashamed when he comes in his own glory and in the glory of the Father and of the holy angels.' "He calls his disciples to 'take up [their] cross and follow [him], for Christ also suffered for [us], leaving [us] an example so that [we] should follow in his steps...' (*CCC 618*).

Q. How did Jesus described a true disciple

St Luke, 6:27-38 and 46-49, describes true disciples as people who love even their enemies and who are willing to do good to those who hate them. They are compassionate even as God the Father is compassionate. They do not judge others or condemn them. They understand that God is the one who judges justly. They are also generous, recognising that all they possess, has been given to them by God. They listen to all that the Lord teaches and they put his teaching into practice.

Matthew, 25:35-40, shows that a true disciple feeds the hungry, gives drink to the thirsty, welcomes strangers, clothes the naked and visits the sick and imprisoned. "...all the faithful, whatever their condition or state - though each in his own way - are called by the Lord to that perfection of sanctity by which the Father himself is perfect." (*CCC 825*). "Incorporated into *Christ* by Baptism, Christians are 'dead to sin and alive to God in Christ Jesus' and so participate in the life of the Risen Lord. Following Christ and united with him, Christians can strive to be 'imitators of God as beloved children, and walk in love' by conforming their thoughts, words and actions to the 'mind... which is yours in Christ Jesus', and by following his example." (*CCC 1694*).

Q. What do we have to do in order to gain eternal life?

We have to respond to the graces God has given to us. "...for man to be able to enter into real intimacy with him, God willed both to reveal himself to man, and to give him the grace of being able to welcome the revelation in faith." (*CCC 35*). "Our justification comes from the grace of God. Grace is *favour, the free and undeserved* help that God gives us to respond to his call to become children of God, adoptive sons, partakers of the divine nature and of eternal life." (*CCC 1996*). "Grace is first and foremost the gift of the Spirit who justifies and sanctifies us..." (*CCC 2003*). "God's free initiative demands *man's free response,* for God has created man in his image by conferring on him, along with freedom, the power to know and love him. The soul only enters freely into the communion of love. God immediately touches and directly moves the heart of man. He has placed in man a longing for truth and goodness that only he can satisfy. The promises of 'eternal life' respond, beyond all hope, to this desire." (*CCC 2002*).

Inspirational People

Q. Can you name a person who showed great love for others
Blessed Martin de Porres [1579-1630] was a Dominican lay brother, born in Peru of a Spanish gentleman and a black slave. He was overseer of the infirmary of a monastery at Lima and showed great love for the poor and the sick. His feast day is November 3rd.

Q. Can you name a person who had a special love for the rejected of society
St Damien dedicated his life to lepers and went to live with them on an island, which had been turned into a leper colony. He eventually contracted the disease himself and died of leprosy.

Q. Why was St Maria Goretti an inspiration for young people
St Maria Goretti [1890-1902] was the daughter of a farm worker of Latium in Italy. She was stabbed to death by a young man. He attacked her and tried to rape her. She was defending her chastity.

POINTS FOR DISCUSSION AND FURTHER ACTIVITIES

LEARNING OBJECTIVE: reflect on what it means to be an inspirational person

Starting Points
The first page of this module in the Pupil's Book gives the important characteristics of an inspirational person. The teacher needs to be aware that pupils are likely to focus on footballers and pop stars who do not necessarily possess the qualities of a follower of Jesus. Ask the pupils to identify the most important words or phrases on page 34 and put them in a spider diagram in their book so that when they come up with the names of inspirational people they can check back to see if they have these characteristics.

Use a glass bowl of water and slowly pour in some more drops to show its ripples - the ripples represent the effect inspirational people can have on others. Have you heard of the BBCs attempt to find the Greatest Briton? Ask the pupils to imagine that they were in charge of the BBC committee, what about a person would help them decide?

Use the story of Aunty Margaret as an example of an ordinary person who is trying to put the teaching of Jesus into practice. Encourage the pupils to reflect on the helpful things other people do for them. What are the qualities we admire in others? Who do we know that is kind and thoughtful towards others? Are there people who have a hard life, but still manage to be cheerful? How can we be inspirational people?

Activities
- Use the worksheet 'People I Admire' page 62, Pupil's Book page 35, or make a worksheet with just one star on your computer. Pupils could put the name of their inspirational person in it and underneath the name write the qualities that the person possesses. Then cut it out and make a mobile to hang up.
- Use the story of 'My brother Michael' page 65 if it would help to give ideas of how to overcome hardships.

Inspirational People

LEARNING OBJECTIVE: know what it means to be a follower of Jesus

Starting Points

In this section we refer back to our Baptism. Jesus is present in us, and if we ask him he will give us the help we need to understand his teaching.

To be a committed Christian is very challenging; it is not a 'soft option'. Being a Christian means making the connection between what we believe and what we do. What does this actually mean for each one of us today? How will it affect the way we treat each other? Will it make a difference to the way we work in class? Is it important that somebody notices that we are making a big effort to be a follower of Jesus? Why/why not?

Activities
- On the computer type the words and phrases that describe what being a Christian involves, enlarge them and display them around the classroom, e.g. Be Compassionate; Do not judge etc. Pupils could think of others e.g. Be kind; Be willing to forgive...
- Invite the pupils to reflect on a time when they were truly Christian and then write about it on a piece of coloured paper so that it could be put up with the enlarged words/phrases in the previous activity.
- Make a decision to live as a 'Very good Christian' for twenty-four hours. For homework, describe what you did and how you felt at the end.
- Watch the video of 'Bahkita, A Wonderful Story', which illustrates all that being a Christian involves.

LEARNING OBJECTIVE: know how Jesus described a true disciple

Starting Points

Note that as you work through this module with the children you are reinforcing the essential teaching of Jesus and relating it to the way we live our life and how we treat others. It is important for pupils to learn to reflect on their behaviour at the end of the morning and afternoon sessions in school. This could take the form of silence for one minute and a short prayer to thank Jesus for helping them through the day. At the start of the morning and afternoon sessions pupils could make an offering to Jesus of all that they are about to do and promise to use all the gifts he has given to them.

When pupils have seen a video clip of 'The House built on Rock' discuss the story with them. What do they think was the main difference between the two houses? What did Jesus say about the man who built his house on rock? What did he say about the other man? What lesson does he want to teach us? What could we do to make sure we lay solid foundations?

Activities
- It may help to relate the parable to the house built on sand to children building sand castles. Make a castle with a plastic beaker of sand and then pour water over it. If possible let the pupils handle the sand. Explain that some people spend their lives building things that only last for a short while. But what Jesus is asking us to build our lives on will be of lasting value - love, compassion, forgiveness etc. Then let pupils feel some large stones and compare what they feel like with the sand. No matter how much water is poured

Inspirational People

over them they will not melt away. This is what our faith in Jesus must be like - no matter what troubles come we will always trust in him.

- Watch the clip of the video 'The Miracle Maker' on the parable of the Two Houses. Or use the video 'Parables for Kids Vol. 2 The House Built on Rock'. Find the story on the Internet 'The Two Builders' *www.ainglkiss.com/teaches/wis.htm*
- Make a list of saintly qualities: Saints :-
- don't just tell you how to live, but show you how;
    - come in all shapes and sizes;
    - come in all ages and races;
    - are sometimes known to us, sometimes not;
    - have big hearts, but not long faces;
    - know that the smallest good deed is better than the biggest good dream;
    - sometimes failed, but never failed to try again;
    - etc.
- Worksheet 'Profile of an Inspirational Person' page 67.
- Worksheets 'Saints on the Web' and 'A Saint who Inspires Me' pages 68, 64 could go together so that information on a saint and a picture could be downloaded from the Internet. The pupils could cut out the picture and stick it onto their own worksheet and use the information in the story to complete the writing frame.
- Pupils could divide a page in two with the title 'Words into Actions'. On one side they could list what Jesus did and on the other side list what their inspirational person does or did. Try to mention about 5 things for each.

LEARNING OBJECTIVE: reflect on the life of a person who showed great love for those rejected by society

Starting Points

It will help pupils to make connections with the teaching of Jesus in Matthew 25:36-45. The day will come for all of us when we die and go before God to give an account of what we have done with the gifts he has given to us. Without dwelling too much on the 'Last Judgement' explain the words of Jesus that when we are kind and helpful towards others, especially those who are poor, lonely and those rejected by most people, we are doing these kind deeds to him.

"For when I was hungry and you gave me food; naked and you clothed me, sick and you visited me, in prison and you came to see me." Then the people asked him, "Lord, when did we see you hungry and feed you; or thirsty and give you drink? When did we see you a stranger and make you welcome; naked and clothe you, sick or in prison and go to see you? Jesus explains "I tell you solemnly, in so far as you did this to one of the least of these brothers of mine, you did it to me" (*Matt* 25:35-40).

Explain how the saints took these words of Jesus seriously. Relate this to the life of Fr Damien and use it as a preparation for the activity on page 47 of Pupil's Book:

Inspirational People

Imagine what happened when Damien died and he met Jesus. Jesus wanted to thank him for all he had done and most especially for putting the Gospel into practice. Work in pairs to write out the conversation between Jesus and Damien.

LEARNING OBJECTIVE: reflect on how we can serve others at home, school, locally, globally. Know that Lent is a time when we can make small sacrifices to show our love for God and others

Starting Points

This is an opportunity to help pupils relate what they are studying about the teaching of Jesus to real life situations at home, in school, in the local community or globally so that they too, can aspire to be inspirational people. Lent is a time when we make a particular effort to be generous to those in need.

Activities

- Watch part two of the video 'Living it Out' - LOVE. This video shows a clip of a young man, Darren, working with the Salvation Army. Ask the pupils to make notes about the reasons Darren gives for working with these people.
- Another clip is the story of the blind beggar, Bartimaeus, sitting at the side of the road and how Jesus healed him - read story Mark 10:46-52. Explain that some people thought Jesus would only talk to important people. But Jesus shows that his main concern was to heal the blind beggar. What does this tell us about Jesus?
- On the same video watch the section that shows the response of a primary school to an earthquake in India. How did the pupils in this school show their concern for the people in India? Why were they particularly keen to help the victims in this earthquake? Is it easy to be concerned about other people? What does it take?
- Action for Lent: Do we know of any situation today where there are people in great need? What could we do about it? How could we involve other people in our school? In groups discuss what could be done. Now draw a shape of your hand and write in the palm what you could do. Cut this shape out and the teacher will put all the hands on a large sheet of paper to display in the classroom. When each person has put their idea in practice their hand could be highlighted.
- Explain to pupils that it is by doing 'good deeds' that we learn how to become inspirational people. Use worksheet 'Plans to become an Inspirational Person' page 69.
- For a Prayerful Reflection for Collective Worship download 'God Knows' from www.ainglkiss.com/bible/knows.htm

Videos

Video 'Living it Out' Christianity in Everyday Life, Grayswood Production Ltd., Willow Grange, Woking Road, Guilford, Surrey GU4 7PZ (Tel. 01483 578967)
Video 'The Miracle Maker' BBC available CTS or St Paul's Multimedia
Video 'Parable for Kids' available St Paul's Multimedia or CTS
Video 'Bakhita A Wonderful Story' St Paul's Multimedia

Inspirational People

Videos 'Saints for Kids' Five volumes, available St Paul's Multimedia or CTS
   Vol. 1: Anne, Joachim, Mary, Joseph, Mark, Andrew & Stephen
   Vol. 2: Elizabeth, Zechariah, Peter, Paul, Cecilia, Benedict, Anthony & Catherine
   Vol. 3: Francis, Clare, Nicholas, Martin, Lucy, John Bosco & Rita
   Vol. 4: Raphael, Luke, Albert, Margaret, Valentine & Ambrose
   Vol. 5: Matthew, Thomas Aquinas, Philip Neri, Frances of Rome, Aloysius Gonzaga & Ida

ICT
see page 68, 'Saints on the Web'.

Additional Resources
The Leprosy Mission International, 80 Windmill Road, Brentford, Middx TW8 OQH Tel. 020 8569 7292
Email *friends@tlmint.org*

4 RECONCILIATION

"There is no limit to God's grace, nor to God's mercy and forgiveness when we fail. Sin is always an exercise of free will. It is always a failure of genuine love of God, of neighbour, of ourselves. Serious (mortal) sin 'separates' us from God until we repent and confess." (RECD p.34)

Reconciliation is a "sacrament of healing. Reconciliation makes sacramentally present Jesus' call to conversion, involves contrition for our sins, confession of them to a priest, and absolution spoken by the priest in the name of Jesus Christ. In the celebration of the sacrament we acknowledge (confess) God's holiness and mercy and are reconciled to God and the community of the Church." (RECD p.24)

Key learning objectives:

AT 1
In this unit you will have the opportunity to:

- know that sin is a failure of love;

- know that when we sin we hurt ourselves and others and damage our relationship with God;

- understand that God loves and forgives us if we are truly sorry;

- know that God heals our friendship with him and others through the Sacrament of Reconciliation;

- know how we can prepare ourselves to receive this Sacrament;

- know what happens during the Sacrament of Reconciliation;

- know that this sacrament enables us to change our behaviour.

AT 2
You will have the chance to:

- reflect on what strengthens our friendship with God and with others and what damages it;

- reflect on times we have shown or been shown love and forgiveness;

- go to confession;

- make the Stations of the Cross.

Reconciliation

THEOLOGICAL INTRODUCTION

Q. What is sin?
"Sin is before all else an offence against God, a rupture of communion with him. At the same time it damages communion with the Church. For this reason conversion entails both God's forgiveness and reconciliation with the Church, which are expressed and accomplished liturgically by the sacrament of Penance and Reconciliation." (*CCC 1440*). "Sin is an offence against reason, truth and right conscience; it is failure in genuine love for God and neighbour caused by perverse attachments to certain goods. It wounds the nature of man and injures human solidarity. It has been defined as 'an utterance, a deed or a desire contrary to the eternal law'." (*CCC 1849*).

Q. What can we do to help ourselves to be sorry for our sins?
"Interior repentance is a radical reorientation of our whole life, a return , a conversion to God with all our heart, an end of sin, a turning away from evil, with repugnance toward the evil actions we have committed. At the same time it entails the desire and resolution to change one's life, with hope in God's mercy and trust in the help of his grace..." (*CCC 1431*). "...This endeavour of conversion is not just a human work. It is the movement of a 'contrite heart' drawn and moved by grace to respond to the merciful love of God who loved us first." (*CCC 1428*).

"...Conversion is first of all a work of the grace of God who makes our hearts return to him: ...God gives us the strength to begin anew. It is in discovering the greatness of God's love that our heart is shaken by the horror and weight of sin and begins to fear offending God by sin and being separated from him. The human heart is converted by looking upon him whom our sins have pierced:

> Let us fix our eyes on Christ's blood and understand how precious it is to his Father, for poured out for our salvation, it has brought to the whole world the grace of repentance." (*CCC 1432*).

Q. Who can forgive sins?
"Only God forgives sins. Since he is the Son of God, Jesus says of himself.' The Son of man has authority on earth to forgive sins', and exercises this divine power: 'Your sins are forgiven.' Further, by virtue of his divine authority he gives this power to men to exercise in his name." (*CCC 1441*). "...he entrusted the exercise of the power of absolution to the apostolic ministry which he charged with the 'ministry of reconciliation'. The apostle is sent out 'on behalf of Christ' with ' God making his appeal' through him and pleading: 'Be reconciled to God.'" (*CCC 1442*).

"In imparting to his apostles his own power to forgive sins the Lord also gives them the authority to reconcile sinners with the Church..." (*CCC 1444*). "...*Reconciliation with the Church is inseparable from reconciliation with God.*" (*CCC 1445*).

Q. What is the Sacrament of Reconciliation?
"The formula of absolution used in the Latin Church expresses the essential elements of this sacrament: The Father of mercies is the source of all forgiveness. He effects the reconciliation of sinners through the Passover of his Son and the gift of his Spirit, through the prayer and ministry of the Church:

Reconciliation

> God the Father of mercies through the death and resurrection of his Son
> has reconciled the world to himself
> and sent the Holy Spirit among us for the forgiveness of sins;
> through the ministry of the Church may God give your pardon and peace,
> and I absolve you from your sins
> in the name of the Father, and of the Son, and of the Holy Spirit." (*CCC 1449*).

Q. How do we prepare ourselves to receive the Sacrament?
"The reception of this sacrament ought to be prepared for by an *examination of conscience* made in the light of the Word of God. The passages best suited to this can be found in the Ten Commandments, and the moral catechesis of the Gospels and the apostolic Letters, such as the Sermon on the Mount and the apostolic teachings." (*CCC 1454*).

Q. What happens during the Sacrament of Reconciliation?
In confession the priest greets the penitent who then makes confession of sins. "Confession to a priest is an essential part of the sacrament of Penance: 'All mortal sins of which penitents after a diligent self-examination are conscious must be recounted by them in confession,...'" (*CCC 1456*).

"Many sins wrong our neighbour. One must do what is possible to repair the harm (e.g., return stolen goods, restore the reputation of someone slandered, pay compensation for injuries)... But sin also injures and weakens the sinner himself, as well as his relationships with God and neighbour. Absolution takes away sin, but it does not remedy all the disorders sin has caused. Raised up from sin, the sinner must still recover his full spiritual health by doing something more to make amends for the sin: he must 'make satisfaction for' or 'expiate' his sins. The satisfaction is also called 'penance'." (*CCC 1459*). The priest then gives absolution and the penitent goes forth in the peace of Christ.

Q. What must we do after receiving this Sacrament?
We must carry out the penance, which the priest has given us. "...The satisfaction we make for our sins, however, is not so much ours as though it were not done through Jesus Christ. We who can do nothing ourselves, as if just by ourselves, can do all things with the co-operation of 'him who strengthens' us. Thus man has nothing of which to boast, but all our boasting is in Christ ...in whom we make satisfaction by bringing forth 'fruits that befit penance'. These fruits have their efficacy from him, by him they are offered to the Father, and through him they are accepted by the Father." (*CCC 1460*).

Q. What are the effects of this Sacrament?
"The whole power of this sacrament of Penance consists in restoring us to God's grace, and joining us with him in an intimate friendship..." (*CCC 1468*). "This sacrament *reconciles us with the Church*. Sin damages or even breaks fraternal communion. The sacrament of Penance repairs or restores it..." (*CCC 1469*).

Summary
Sin disrupts harmony and causes unhappiness. It lowers the quality of life. It harms and can destroy the life of grace, which is God's most wonderful gift. We cannot heal ourselves of sin. Only God can forgive sins

Reconciliation

and restore grace. We must, therefore, pray for forgiveness when we sin and take our sins to be forgiven by God, through the ministry of the Church, in the Sacrament of Reconciliation, which our Lord so lovingly instituted to save us from despair.

POINTS FOR DISCUSSION AND FURTHER ACTIVITIES

LEARNING OBJECTIVE: reflect on wrong choices and the consequences of our actions

Starting Points

Explain to the pupils that for the next few weeks they are going to reflect on their behaviour and how it affects others. Take time to make links with the work already covered this year: God's gifts to us; God gives us the Commandments and sends his Son, Jesus, to show us how to live a good life; this is followed by lots of examples of inspirational people who have put the teaching of Jesus into practice and now it is over to us to reflect on the way we live.

Discuss the poem 'Please Sir' (Pupil's Book page 48) with the pupils. Are these situations likely to happen in your school? How would they feel if they were the teacher? Do they think it would be easy to be a Duty Teacher? Why? What happens in this class that makes life difficult for the teacher? What can they do about it? Why is it important that they try to help each other?

LEARNING OBJECTIVE: know that sin hurts us, others and our relationship with God

Starting Points

It is important to make connections here with the story of the 'Fall' and 'Original Sin' in the first section. Because of original sin there is a tendency within us to be selfish etc. This is why God sent his Son, Jesus, to help us.

It is very important to give time for pupils to reflect on the content of this section. It may help to settle them into a 'prayer circle' to think about the situations where things have gone wrong.

In the story of the **Prodigal Son** it is important to stress that the main point of the story is the unconditional love of the father. The father is so eager to forgive his son that he looks out for him every day. Jesus says God is like this - not only is he willing to forgive people, but he is actually longing for them to come to him. The giving of the clothes, sandals and ring is to show that the son is welcomed back as a member of the family.

Additional Activities
- Teacher provides pieces of paper, elastic bands and stones. Pupils write down the wrong choices that people make (not personal things). The pieces of paper are put around the stone and secured with the elastic band. Then they are all put into one big bag and pupils feel the weight. Use this to give an idea of what it feels like when we have done something wrong and how it weighs on our mind until we confess it. These pieces of paper are then removed from the stones, nobody reads them, they are put through a shredder or taken outside and burnt.

Reconciliation

- Fold a sheet of paper in two. Cut out the shape of a person so that it becomes two people and they are holding hands. Then invite a child to tear them apart. This what sin does to our relationships, it damages the friendship so that they can no longer feel close. Stick the two shapes onto the board with a gap between them. Ask the children to suggest the 'hurt feelings' that there are between the two people and put them on 'post its' in the gap.
- End these lessons with a prayer asking Jesus to forgive us e.g.

    Dear Jesus,
    We thank you for being present with us.
    Help us today to forgive all those who have hurt us.
    Forgive us for anything we have done wrong and help to be to kind to anyone we have hurt. Amen.

The Prodigal Son
- Ask the children to look at the picture in the Pupil's Book page 56 while you read the story. What are the following people showing by their body language: the mother is like the shape of a cross (*she has suffered*); the older brother has his arms folded (*bitterness*); the father has his arms outstretched (*welcome*); the son has his arms and head down (*shame*)
- Look at the colours: red - warm welcome, suffering; yellow - joy, excited; grey - sorrow, repentance; mustard - jealousy.
- Notice the distance between the people: the dog jumps straight up, he has not been hurt; the father has a small gap between him and the son, he is ready to forgive, but there is that little gap to be crossed. Notice where the elder brother is. Is he reluctant to forgive? Notice the rider in the distance - what do you think are the thoughts going through his head?
- Explain that forgiveness crosses the gap of hurt feelings. The father welcoming the son with open arms is a reminder that God always forgives the sinner no matter what he/she has done as long as that person turns back to him and seeks forgiveness.
- Watch the section of the video 'Living it Out' on the Prodigal Son.
    Or Parables for Kids Vol. 1 The Prodigal Son
    Or Parables for Kids Vol. 2 The Man with Two Sons
- Work in groups of three.
    a) Think of a modern day parable of a 'lost son or daughter'.
        - Imagine someone who left home because he/she wanted more freedom.
        - Did this person find happiness?
        - Did he/she have enough money to live on?
        - What happened then?
        - What kind of welcome did this person get on returning home?
    b) Write a play about this person that you could dramatise for the class.
        Make sure that there is a message in it for us about how we should treat others.

LEARNING OBJECTIVE: understand that God loves us and forgives us if we are truly sorry

Starting Points

In the section 'Forgiveness is not easy!' it may help to have 'circle prayer' so as to give the children an opportunity to reflect on the important ideas here. Invite the children to imagine a situation rather than make it personal.

Reconciliation

Explain that Jesus did not literally mean that we forgive 77 times. Seven is a symbolic number: he just meant, 'Go on forgiving', but it does not mean that we should repeatedly forgive somebody who is hurting us. The person being forgiven must show that they are trying to change their behaviour. That is why we have to have a firm purpose of amendment when we do something wrong.

In the quotation from John 15:10 *"If you remain in me and my words remain in you, you may ask what you will and you shall get it"* - it is important to explain to the pupils that this is not a Father Christmas type of situation. To *'remain in Jesus'* and for his words to remain in us, we have to be living in very close union with him. All things will work out for our good in the end, but it may not be the way we think it should. We may be asking for something that would lead us away from God rather than bring us closer to him - if that is the case, he will not grant what we want, but he will lead us in the right path.

Additional Activities
- Watch clip of video 'Living it Out' on Forgiveness - it explains why forgiveness is not easy.
- Discuss: What would you say to someone who wants to 'get even' - link it to the words of the 'Our Father': *'forgive us our trespasses as we forgive those who trespass against us'*.
- Describe a situation where a pupil is being bullied in school. Explain that it is not kindness to put up with a bully; forgiveness does not mean tolerating evil. In order to forgive it is necessary to make certain demands of the person who has done wrong.

LEARNING OBJECTIVE: understand the importance of the Sacrament of Reconciliation.
Go to Confession

Starting Points

It is important to remember that some pupils may have an under-active conscience and others may have an over-active one, so it needs to be informed. Explain that it is a little voice deep inside us, when we think about what we are going to do - it may help us to feel good about ourselves or it may make us feel guilty. It is a little like God's alarm bell. It is a feeling inside to help us to do what is right and avoid what is wrong.

If it is at all possible try to provide an opportunity for pupils to go to Confession. If you want to invite a priest to come into school be sure to give him plenty of notice so that he can plan it well in advance.

Activities
- Worksheet on 'My Conscience' page 73.
- The story of Zachaeus was covered in Book 3. Recap on the story by reading Luke 19:1-10 and then use worksheet page 74.
- Use website *www.ainglkiss.com/xam4kids/* to give pupils help with an examination of conscience.
- Take the pupils out to a church to see the confessional and if possible, arrange for a priest to be there to hear their confession.

Reconciliation

LEARNING OBJECTIVE: make the Stations of the Cross

Starting Points

It helps pupils if the passion, death and resurrection of Jesus is presented in a different way each year. In Year 5 it is suggested that the focus should be on the Stations of the Cross. The best way to do this is to take the pupils out to a church and make the Stations of the Cross with them. CTS or St Paul's will have very simple booklets on the Stations for guidance.

Additional Activities

- For material on the Stations of the Cross look at the following websites:
  www.cptryon.org/prayer/child/stations/01.htm
  www.ainglkiss.com/stations/4kids
  www.topmarks.co.uk/christianity/easter.htm
- Use the worksheet with just the pictures of the Stations of the Cross, page 75, and get the pupils to write beside each station what is happening.
- Use video clip of 'The Miracle Maker' or 'Jesus of Nazareth' on the crucifixion as a preparation for going out to church to make the stations.
- The Signs of the Cross can also be made in the classroom with the pupils making the pictures and writing the reflections and the teacher providing the traditional prayers. The Pictures and reflections can be made into a book later. Alternatively the Stations can be made as a whole school activity in the hall with children from each class performing a tableau while others read meditations and prayers.

Videos

The Miracle Maker - BBC
Video 'Living it Out' Christianity in Everyday Life, Grayswood Production Ltd., Willow Grange, Woking Road, Guilford, Surrey GU4 7PZ (Tel. 01483 578967)
Parables for Kids, Vol. 1 & 2 St Paul's Multimedia or CTS

Reconciliation

Guided Meditation
Jesus is always ready to forgive us

I would like to invite you to close your eyes, put both feet on the ground, you can sit up straight or put your head down on the table.

Imagine you have found a quiet place to be alone, a place where you can be safe and still, you just want to be very peaceful.
(Pause)
After a while you notice that you are not alone.
Not far from you Jesus is sitting with his head lowered... he is praying. He knows that you are there as well.

He invites you to come and sit with him. He asks you why you are here. You tell him that you want to think about all that has been happening, in particular some of the things that upset you and then you have the courage to tell him that you have upset others as well. You tell him that it is like having a heavy bag of stones on your back.
(Pause)
Jesus smiles, he knows how you are feeling, he also knows that you want to put things right. He says that people worry about their mistakes; they worry about the people they have hurt. You know just what he is talking about; it is as if he can read your mind.

Jesus explains that he is always ready to forgive anyone who is sorry for what they have done wrong. This is why he has given us the Sacrament of Reconciliation. Everyone can receive this Sacrament as often as they wish, even if they have not committed real sin, because it gives them the grace to grow stronger and always to choose the right thing to do.

Jesus knows how hard I try to be good, to be helpful and kind towards and he thanks me for all my efforts. I then spend a few minutes telling Jesus about the things that are deep in my heart...
(Pause)
It is time now to leave this wonderful place. I say goodbye to Jesus. I feel very peaceful now.

When you are ready open your eyes and wait for the rest of the class to join you.

5 LIFE IN THE RISEN JESUS

"Prayer is a living relationship with God in, with and through Jesus Christ; an encounter which takes place in the intimacy of the heart of each person. All prayer, whether private or public is God's gift, the action of the holy Spirit in us and an expression of this living relationship. Prayer is an expression of the universal search for God and of the response of faith to God's Self-Revelation." (RECD p.25)

Key learning objectives:

AT 1
In this unit you will have the opportunity to:

- know and understand that Jesus is risen from the dead;

- know the story of the appearance of Jesus to Mary of Magdala; [John 20:11-18]

- know that the risen Jesus is present among us in different ways;

- know Jesus' teaching and example on prayer;

- know and understand the 'Our Father';

- know that we can pray in different ways;

- learn to pray the Rosary;

- know the Glorious Mysteries and how they help us to think about the Resurrection of Jesus.

AT 2
You will have the chance to:

- appreciate that Jesus is present in our lives;

- recognise the importance of making time for prayer each day;

- reflect on the meaning of some traditional prayers, e.g. 'Our Father';

- experience a guided meditation on the Resurrection.

Life in the Risen Jesus

THEOLOGICAL INTRODUCTION

Q. How do we know and what does it mean to say that Jesus rose from the dead?

"The mystery of Christ's resurrection is a real event, with manifestations that were historically verified, as the New Testament bears witness." (*CCC 639*). "The empty tomb and the linen cloths lying there signify in themselves that by God's power Christ's body had escaped the bonds of death and corruption. They prepared the disciples to encounter the Risen Lord." (*CCC 657*).

"By means of touch and the sharing of a meal, the risen Jesus establishes direct contact with his disciples. He invites them in this way to recognise that he is not a ghost and above all to verify that the risen body in which he appears to them is the same body that had been tortured and crucified, for it still bears the traces of his Passion. Yet at the same time this authentic, real body possesses the new properties of a glorious body: not limited by space and time but able to be present how and when he wills; for Christ's humanity can no longer be confined to earth, and belongs henceforth only to the Father's divine realm. For this reason too the risen Jesus enjoys the sovereign freedom of appearing as he wishes: in the guise of a gardener or in other forms familiar to his disciples, precisely to awaken their faith." (*CCC 645*).

"Christ's resurrection was not a return to earthly life, as was the case with the raisings from the dead that he had performed before Easter: Jairus' daughter, the young man of Naim, Lazarus... Christ's resurrection is essentially different. In his risen body he passes from the state of death to another life beyond time and space. At Jesus' Resurrection his body is filled with the power of the Holy Spirit: he shares the divine life in his glorious state, so that St Paul can say that Christ is 'the man of heaven'." (*CCC 646*). "Faith in the Resurrection has as its object an event which is historically attested to by the disciples, who really encountered the Risen One. At the same time, this event is mysteriously transcendent insofar as it is the entry of Christ's humanity into the glory of God." (*CCC 656*).

Q. Where do we find the story of the appearance of Jesus to Mary of Magdala

"Mary Magdalene and the holy women who came to finish anointing the body of Jesus, which had been buried in haste because the Sabbath began on the evening of Good Friday, were the first to encounter the Risen One. Thus the women were the first messengers of Christ's Resurrection for the apostles themselves." (See *Mark* 16:9-11. For a detailed account of an appearance of our Lord to Mary of Magdala, see *John* 20:11-18).

Q. In what ways is the Risen Jesus present among us today?

"'Christ is always present in his Church, especially in her liturgical celebrations. He is present in the Sacrifice of the Mass not only in the person of his minister, 'the same now offering, through the ministry of priests, who formerly offered himself on the cross', but especially in the Eucharistic species. By his power he is present in the sacraments so that when anyone baptises it is really Christ himself who baptises. He is present in his word since it is he himself who speaks when the holy Scriptures are read in the Church. Lastly, he is present when the Church prays and sings, for he has promised 'where two or three are gathered in my name there am I in the midst of them.' (*CCC 1088*).

Life in the Risen Jesus

Q. When did Jesus pray?

"...Jesus prays *before* the decisive moments of his mission: before his Father's witness to him during his Baptism and Transfiguration, and before his own fulfillment of the Father's plan of love by his Passion. He also prays before the decisive moments involving the mission of his apostles: at the election and call of the Twelve, before Peter's confession of him as 'the Christ of God', and again that the faith of the chief of the apostles may not fail when tempted. Jesus' prayer before the events of salvation that the Father has asked him to fulfill is a humble and trusting commitment of his human will to the loving will of his Father." (*CCC 2600, see also 2602 to 2606*).

Q. What did Jesus teach about prayer?

"When Jesus prays he is already teaching us how to pray... But the Gospel also gives us Jesus' explicit teaching on prayer..." (*CCC 2607*). "From the *Sermon on the Mount* onwards, Jesus insists on *conversion of heart:* reconciliation with one's brother before presenting an offering on the altar, love of enemies and prayer for persecutors, prayer to the Father in secret, not heaping up empty phrases, prayerful forgiveness from the depths of the heart, purity of heart and seeking the kingdom before all else. This filial conversion is entirely directed to the Father." (*CCC 2608*).

"Once committed to conversion, the heart learns to pray in *faith*. Faith is a filial adherence to God beyond what we feel and understand. It is possible because the beloved Son gives us access to the Father. He can ask us to 'seek' and to 'knock', since he himself is the door and the way." (*CCC 2609*). "...he teaches us *filial boldness:* 'Whatever you ask in prayer, believe that you will receive it, and you will'." (*CCC 2610*). "The prayer of faith consists not only in saying 'Lord, Lord', but in disposing the heart to do the will of the Father..." (*CCC 2611*)

Q. What are the different ways in which we can pray?

"...Jesus teaches us a vocal prayer, the *Our Father*. He not only prayed aloud the liturgical prayers of the synagogue but as the gospels show, he raised his voice to express his personal prayer, from exultant blessing of the Father to the agony of Gethsemane." (*CCC 2701*).

"Meditation is above all a quest. The mind seeks to understand the why and how of the Christian life, in order to adhere and respond to what the Lord is asking... We are usually helped by books... the Sacred Scriptures, particularly the Gospels..." (*CCC 2705*). "Christian prayer tries above all to meditate on the mysteries of Christ, as in *lectio divina* or the rosary..." (*CCC 2708*).

"Contemplative prayer is the prayer of the child of God, of the forgiven sinner who agrees to welcome the love by which he is loved and who wants to respond to it by loving even more. But he knows that the love he is returning is poured out by the Spirit in his heart, for everything is grace from God. Contemplative prayer is the poor and humble surrender to the loving will of the Father in ever deeper union with his beloved Son." (*CCC 2712*).

Q. What is the Rosary?

"Medieval piety in the West developed the prayer of the rosary as a popular substitute for the Liturgy of the Hours..." (*CCC 2678*). It consists in praying the Our Father followed by the Hail Mary ten times and then the glory be, while thinking on various events, mainly in our Lord's life. These events are divided into the

Life in the Risen Jesus

Joyful Mysteries, Luminous Mysteries, Sorrowful Mysteries and Glorious Mysteries. For additional information see Apostolic Letter *Rosarium Virginis Mariae* Pope John Paul II, CTS 2002.

POINTS FOR DISCUSSION AND FURTHER ACTIVITIES

LEARNING OBJECTIVE: know and understand that Jesus is risen from the dead

Starting Points

Set the Scene: Replace any pictures of Good Friday from the display boards with pictures of the Resurrection, symbols of new life, joy and spring. It would be good to have a prayer corner and a paschal candle or a large candle.

This module provides opportunities to make links with what pupils have already studied so that the death and resurrection of Jesus is not an isolated event but is linked to the celebration of Mass and the other sacraments. The news of the Resurrection of Jesus gives new meaning and purpose to our life - he has conquered death, even though people die, they will rise again and enjoy eternal life with him in heaven. Because Jesus is risen from the dead he is present in our world today - this will be developed later in this module.

Recall the events of Good Friday. Recall how the disciples had seen their master die on a cross. Ask the pupils how they think the disciples felt? Did they think it was the end? Did any of them believe he would rise again? [*It is unlikely that the disciples would remember some of the promises Jesus had made, they were probably feeling that all their hopes had been in vain because the Saviour in whom they had put their trust had died.*]

Simplified stories of the Resurrection: Pupil's Book 3 'The disciples on the road to Emmaus' pages 66-67; 'Doubting Thomas' pages 68-69.

Additional Activities
- For a brief and simple resume of Good Friday and Easter Sunday log on to
www.ainglkiss.com/stories/eas.htm 'Where is Jesus' & 'Jesus Returns'.
- Discuss the events of the Resurrection with the pupils before doing the activities. Encourage children to 'think' rather than just recall events.
    - What do they think happened to the body of Jesus? Was it stolen? Who would be likely to steal it? Why?
    - The soldiers guarding the tomb had fallen asleep - what do you think will happen to them for not doing their duty?
    - Could it have been a ghost that Mary of Magdala saw? Why, why not? What evidence does she give? Do you believe her story?
- Encourage the pupils to develop their higher order skills e.g.
    - Predicting: When the women came to tell the other disciples that Jesus was alive - what are the different responses they could have made?
    - Analysing: What are the different stories about the resurrection telling us?
    - Deducing: If it is true that Jesus rose from the dead, then it means that we...

Life in the Risen Jesus

- Evaluating: How important are the stories of the resurrection for us today?
- Show clip of the Resurrection appearances from the video 'The Miracle Maker'. See page 70 of BBC Activity Book for further activities.
- Read the story of Jesus meeting the disciples on the shore of Tiberias (*John* 21:1-14) as this may be the first time the pupils have heard it.
- Scripture text and worksheet 'Prepare to Meet the Police!' page 76. Some of the scripture passages (which can be found on *www.tere.org* under 'Support Material') are very short and others long - this allows for differentiation.
- Worksheet page 77 to write an article for the front page of the local newspaper.
- See Guided Meditation 'Do You Love Me' John 21:4-17 page 44.

LEARNING OBJECTIVE: know that Jesus is present among us in different ways

Starting Points

This section provided a good opportunity to make links with what has been covered in Years 3 & 4: revise briefly the Sacrament of Baptism, the Sacrament of Reconciliation and the Mass.

Explain the great gift that Jesus gives us in the Eucharist: each time we go to Mass we can receive him in Holy Communion. The consecrated hosts, which remain after we have received Holy Communion, are placed in the tabernacle. We call these hosts the Blessed Sacrament. When you see a sanctuary lamp burning in a Catholic church this is a sign that the Blessed Sacrament is in the tabernacle. That is why we genuflect when we enter the church and why so many people like to spend time praying before the Blessed Sacrament. We know that Jesus is truly present in the Blessed Sacrament.

Additional Activities
- Invite the children to share, first of all with one another then with the class, what they learned about Baptism, Reconciliation and the Mass. It is worth spending some time on each of the Sacraments so that they will deepen their understanding of them and make connections with what they are now studying.
- Pupils could bring in photos of their Baptism or First Holy Communion as focal points for conversation.
- Use the picture of the Prayer Symbol page 78 for discussion, for example:
    - What does the drawing make you think about?
    - What do you think they are saying to each other?
    - What can you tell about the two figures from their bodies?
    - How many lines has the artist used? Is that important? (From Cracking RE Issue 12)
- Lead children into a short meditation with Jesus. Explain that in this meditation we think about Jesus, believing that he is with us.
    - We sit quietly, close our eyes; we place our hands in our lap with the palms facing up. We think about Jesus placing his hands in ours and asking us just to sit quietly with him. We know he loves us and we try to tell him how much we love him.
    - Breathe slowly and deeply. Be aware of each breath you take. As you inhale, feel Jesus' love coming into your heart. As you exhale, softly say the name Jesus. Know that Jesus is with you here and now.
    - Thank Jesus for coming to you and ask him to help you and to help other people for whom you want to pray.

Life in the Risen Jesus

LEARNING OBJECTIVE: know there are different ways of praying

Starting Points

It is important for the children to see you, the teacher, as a person who prays. The habit of praying develops through practice. It is our tradition to begin prayer by making the sign of the cross. This is a reminder that we are putting ourselves in the presence of God.

One of the best ways to help children know and understand different ways of praying is to provide opportunities for them to experience a variety of ways. Here are some examples:
We pray together in school at the start of the day. This could take the form of petition, thanksgiving or praise etc. If we sing a hymn we are praising God. At home we pray with our families at meal times and before we go to sleep. When we go to Mass we take part in the prayer of the whole Church in the celebration of the Eucharist.

Additional Activities
- Provide an opportunity for pupils to experience a meditation on a scripture passage, see page 44.
- If possible take pupils out to the parish church to pray in silence before the Blessed Sacrament - prayer of contemplation. Organise Benediction if possible, either in Church or School.
- For more help on prayer go to *www.cptryon.org/prayer/child/easterhp/index.html* 'When we pray, we connect with God'.
- For every-day prayers and prayers of the Church go to: *www.cptryon.org/prayer/child/index.html*
- Encourage pupils to make their own Prayer Book. If you send it to CTS for the Editor of this book before the end of July in any year the best will be selected and put on the website *www.tere.org*

LEARNING OBJECTIVE: reflect on Jesus' teaching and example on prayer. Know and understand the Our Father

Starting Points

Jesus gives us clear instructions about praying because he wants us to have a close, personal relationship with him. So when we pray we are not doing it because others will see us. (*Matt* 6:5-6).

When Jesus says: 'Do not babble as the pagans do' he is speaking of people who worship many gods and think that by praying they can manipulate them. They use lots of words because they are afraid to omit any part of a request in case they offend the gods. We do not need to use a lot of words because God already knows our inmost thoughts and desires.

Explain that the disciples often saw Jesus in prayer and one day they asked him to teach them how to pray. This is when he taught them the 'Our Father'. The word he used for 'father' actually means 'daddy'. It shows that Jesus had a very close relationship with God his Father and he wants us to have the same.

Additional Activities
- For a simple version of 'The Pharisee and the Tax Collector' go to *www.ainglkiss.com/teaches/tax.htm*
- Show video of 'The Pharisee and the Tax Collector' Parables for Kids Vol. 1

Life in the Risen Jesus

- Show clip of video 'Living it Out Part 3 Forgiveness' where there are children in a Catholic Church singing the 'Our Father' and putting actions to it. Are there ideas here that the pupils could use for assembly?
- For a very good explanation of the 'Our Father' go to *www.cptryon.org/prayer/child/father.html*
- For morning and night prayers see page 79.

LEARNING OBJECTIVE: Learn how to pray the Rosary

Starting Points

The most obvious way to show pupils how to say the rosary is to say it with them. You could choose to say one decade a week for 5 weeks.

It will be helpful to let children know something about the devotion to the Rosary in the history of the Church. For example, the message of Our Lady to the children of Fatima:
Our Lady asked them to say the rosary every day to earn peace for the world and the end of the war. On another occasion the Lady told Lucia, "I want to tell you that they must build a chapel here in my honour, that I am the Lady of the Rosary and that people must continue to pray the rosary everyday. The war will end and the soldiers will return to their homes soon." [*The History and Devotion of the Rosary* - R. Gribble C.S.C page 154.]

Additional Activities
- Work in pairs. Imagine you are going to have a meeting with Mary, Our Mother.
  a) Think of five questions you would like to ask her about the events connected with the Glorious Mysteries.
  b) Interview a partner, using your questions. (Make sure you record their answers.)
  c) Once you have done this, swap over and let your partner be the interviewer.
  d) Write an article for a newspaper about this interview.
- Worksheet page 82 Match the Mysteries with their meanings.
- For an explanation of the meaning of the Mysteries of the Rosary go to
www.cptryon.org/prayer/child/index.html and click on 'A Scriptural Rosary'.

ICT

www.ainglkiss.com/stories/eas.htm 'Where is Jesus' & 'Jesus Returns'
www.ainglkiss.com/teaches/tax.htm 'The Pharisee & the Tax Collector'
www.cptryon.org/prayer/child/father.html Explanation of the Our Father
www.cptryon.org/prayer/child/easterhp/index.html When we pray, we 'connect' with God
www.ainglkiss.com/rosary4kids/ The Rosary for Kids
www.ainglkiss.com/ros/krdia.htm Diagram of the Rosary
cmri.org/message.htm The Fatima Message

Videos

The Miracle Maker: Clip of the Resurrection appearances
Parables for Kids Vol. 1 'The Pharisee and the Tax Collector'
'Living it Out' - Section on 'Forgiveness' for the 'Our Father'

Life in the Risen Jesus

A Guided Meditation: John 21:4-17
Do You Love Me?

It is a lovely sunny morning with a gentle warm breeze blowing on the seashore. You have come out early because you want to think about all the things that were happening. You can hear the cry of the seagulls as they hover overhead looking for fish. There is a fishing boat that looks as if it is coming in, but apart from that you are alone watching the waves and making your footprints on the wet sand.

After a while you notice a man who has lit a fire on the seashore. He smiles at you as if he knows you. You recognise his face, but you are not sure who he is. Then, suddenly you realise it is Jesus; he invites you to join him. He tells you that he is preparing breakfast for his friends and would like you to stay to meet them.

Then he goes over to the edge of the water and calls out to the men in the fishing boat. 'Have you caught anything, friends?' And when they answered, 'No', he says, 'Throw the net out to starboard and you'll find something'. From where you're sitting, you can see that they do what they are told and immediately the fish pile into the net.

Jesus no sooner returns to the fire when, someone comes running towards him. It's Simon Peter, he is very excited: he knows it is Jesus and because of this he has jumped out of the boat, straight into the sea with his clothes on - he could not wait to get to Jesus. Soon a few more disciples arrive.

After the meal Jesus says to Simon Peter: 'Simon, son of John, do you love me more than these others do?' He answers, 'Yes Lord, you know I love you'. Jesus says to him, 'Feed my lambs.' A second time he says to him 'Simon, son of John do you love me?' He replies, 'Yes, Lord, you know I love you'. Jesus says to him, 'Look after my sheep'. Then he says to him a third time, 'Simon son of John, do you love me?' Peter is upset that he asks him the third time, 'Do you love me?' and says, 'Lord you know everything; you know I love you', Jesus says to him, 'Feed my sheep'.

Then Jesus turns to you, it is as if his eyes can see right into your heart, he calls you by name and asks, 'Do you love me?' What is your reply? It is a very powerful and wonderful experience: you talk to Jesus and listen carefully to what he says to you. Now you just want to be quiet for a little while to think about it all.

6 PEOPLE OF OTHER FAITHS

"All nations are one community and have one origin, because God caused the whole human race to dwell on the face of the earth. They also have one final end, God, whose providence, manifestation of goodness and plans for salvation are extended to all." (*Nostrae Aetate,* para 1)

"The Catholic Church rejects nothing of those things which are true and holy in these religions. It regards with respect those ways of acting and living and those precepts and teachings which, though often at variance with what it holds and expounds, frequently reflect a ray of truth which enlightens everyone... It therefore calls upon all its sons and daughters with prudence and charity, through dialogue and co-operation with the followers of other religions, bearing witness to the Christian faith and way of life, to **recognise**, **preserve** and **promote** those spiritual and moral good things as well as the socio-cultural values which are to be found among them." (*Nostrae Aetate* para 2)

Key learning objectives:

AT 1
In this unit you will have the opportunity to:

- know that we live in a country where people have different beliefs and different cultures;

- know that Christianity comes from Judaism;

- know that there are other faiths e.g. Islam/ Hinduism;

- know what we share in common with other faiths, e.g. Islam/ Hinduism;

- know what some of the differences are between Christianity and other faiths, e.g.Islam/ Hinduism;

- know what the Catholic Church teaches about our relations with other faiths;

- know that all religions have special celebrations and times for prayer.

AT 2
You will have the chance to:

- reflect on how we treat others with different beliefs from ours;

- appreciate what we have in common with people of other faiths;

- find out what your friends/neighbours believe.

People of Other Faiths

THEOLOGICAL INTRODUCTION

Q. What is the relationship between Judaism and Christianity?
"At all times and in every race, anyone who fears God and does what is right has been acceptable to him. He has, however, willed to make men holy... to make them into a people who might acknowledge him and serve him in holiness. He therefore chose the Israelite race to be his own people and established a covenant with it. He gradually instructed this people... All things, however, happened as a preparation for and figure of that new and perfect covenant which was to be ratified in Christ... the New Covenant in his blood; he called together a race made up of Jews and Gentiles which would be one, not according to the flesh, but in the Spirit." (*CCC 781*).

Christianity, therefore, grew out of Judaism and brought it to fulfilment in the New Covenant. Jesus was born a Jew but created the new people of God, not as a particular race, but as a people filled with his Spirit. "*The relationship of the Church with the Jewish People:* When she delves into her own mystery, the Church, the People of God in the New Covenant, discovers her link with the Jewish People, the first to hear the Word of God. The Jewish faith, unlike other non-Christian religions is already a response to God's revelation in the Old Covenant. To the Jews 'belong the sonship, the glory, the covenants, the giving of the law, the worship, and the promises; to them belong the patriarchs, and of their race, according to the flesh, is the Christ'; for the gifts and the call of God are irrevocable.'" (*CCC 839*).

Q. Why do Catholics believe that there is only one true faith?
"God has revealed himself fully by sending his own Son, in whom he has established his covenant for ever. The Son is his Father's definitive Word; so there will be no further Revelation after him." (*CCC 73*). "Through the centuries, in so many languages, cultures, peoples and nations, the Church has constantly confessed the one faith, received from the one Lord, transmitted by one Baptism, and grounded in the conviction that all people have only one God and Father..." (*CCC 172*).

Q. What is culture?
"Culture is an organised way of life based on a common tradition, and conditioned by a common environment... Every culture represents a spiritual community and involves common beliefs and common ways of thought... The cultural function of religion is both conservative and dynamic: it consecrates the tradition of a culture and it also provides the common aim which unifies the different social elements in a culture..." ('*Religion and Culture*' by Christopher Dawson, p.46).

Q. What different beliefs and cultures are to be found in our country?
Q. How does the Church regard these different beliefs?
There are Christians who have different beliefs. There are also non-Christian religions, Muslims, Sikhs, Buddhists and so on. There are different cultures also: West Indian, Arabic, Chinese, and so on. "'The Church knows that she is joined in many ways to the baptised who are honoured by the name of Christian, but do not profess the Catholic faith in its entirety or have not preserved unity or communion under the successor of St Peter.' Those 'who believe in Christ and have been properly baptised are put in a certain, although imperfect, communion with the Catholic Church.' *With the Orthodox Churches*, this communion

is so profound 'that it lacks little to attain the fullness that would permit a common celebration of the Lord's Eucharist.'" *(CCC 838)*.

"The Church's relationship with the Muslims. The plan of salvation also includes those who acknowledge the Creator, in the first place amongst whom are the Muslims; these profess to hold the faith of Abraham, and together with us they adore the one, the merciful God, mankind's judge on the last day.'" *(CCC 841)*.

"The Catholic Church recognises in other religions that search, among shadows and images, for the God who is unknown yet near since he gives life and breath and all things, and wants all men to be saved. Thus the Church considers all goodness and truth found in these religions as 'a preparation for the Gospel, and given by him who enlightens all men that they may at length have life'." *(CCC 843)*.

Q. What features are common to religions?
All religions will have certain beliefs. They will have ways of worshipping God and common ways of praying. They will have places for worship. They will celebrate feastdays. They will have religious customs and rules and commandments, which govern the lives of the faithful.

Q. How should Catholics act towards people of other faiths?
"...Christ always gives his Church the gift of unity, but the Church must always pray and work to maintain, reinforce and perfect the unity that Christ wills for her... The desire to recover the unity of all Christians is a gift of Christ and a call of the Holy Spirit." *(CCC 820)*. "Certain things are required in order to respond adequately to this call: - a permanent *renewal* of the Church in greater fidelity to her vocation... - *conversion of heart* as the faithful 'try to live holier lives according to the Gospel', for it is the unfaithfulness of the members to Christ's gift which causes divisions; *prayer in common... - fraternal knowledge of each other...*" and so on. *(CCC 821)*.

"Concern for achieving unity 'involves the whole Church, faithful and clergy alike.' But we must realise 'that this holy objective... transcends human powers and gifts'. That is why we place all our hope 'in the prayer of Christ for the Church, in the love of the Father for us, and in the power of the Holy Spirit'." *(CCC 822)*. Catholics must also remember that "'Nobody may be forced to act against his convictions, nor is anyone to be restrained from acting in accordance with his conscience in religious matters in private or in public, alone or in association with others, within due limits.' This right is based on the very nature of the human person, whose dignity enables him freely to assent to the divine truth, which transcends the temporal order. For this reason 'it continues to exist even in those who do not live up to their obligation of seeking the truth and adhering to it.'" *(CCC 2106)*.

The Catholic Church acknowledges that it is in constant need of reform and renewal as far as the 'expression and form' of faith goes - but not in substance. The latter remains unchanged.

People of Other Faiths

POINTS FOR DISCUSSION AND FURTHER ACTIVITIES

LEARNING OBJECTIVE: know that we live in a country where people have different cultures

Starting Points

It may help to introduce this module by highlighting that we are a nation of immigrants. Many families with British sounding names may have come to Britain recently and may people whose names sound foreign to us would actually have been born here.

Activities
- Words for Glossary:
  Halal: food or clothing which is proper for a Muslim
  Kosher: food that is fit to be eaten by an observant Jew is classified as kosher
  Tandoori: food cooked over charcoal
- Children could research where their family name originated and this could lead to a celebration of all the different countries: prepare by drawing the flags and translating words of 'welcome', finding some music and other things that are characteristic of the country.
- Use a map of the world and put little flags on it to indicate where the different families originated. This could be a focal point for prayer particularly if there is trouble in those parts of the world. During prayer time a candle could be lit for each country suffering from any kind of natural disaster or fighting etc.

LEARNING OBJECTIVE: reflect on different beliefs in our country

Starting Points

It must be clear from the outset that this module is not intended as a study of other religions. There are numerous resources available to cover these religions in depth, so our aim here is only to give a 'snapshot' of them.

Our standpoint is that as Catholics we have to be clear about own identity, what we believe and why. Only then are we in a position to know how we differ from other religions and come to recognise what we have in common and why there are differences among us.

We believe that God created the world so when we look at other religions we see echoes of the Creator in all religions. There are positive things we can learn from them.

For background information for the teacher go to *www.bbc.co.uk/religion/religions/*

The BBC Programmes *Pathways of Belief:* videos and booklets on Judaism, Islam, Hinduism and Sikhism provide excellent material for classroom use. Each programme is based on key beliefs or related concepts.

Additional Activities

It will help to use clips of the following videos when teaching about aspects of other faiths, for example,

People of Other Faiths

Judaism
1 God
2 Torah: A way of life
3 The family

Unit 1 Islam
1 Allah - Creator and Provider
2 Living as a Muslim - Ramadan and daily prayer

Unit 2 Hinduism
1 God - one God, many aspects
2 Living as a Hindu - new beginnings and Divali

Unit 3 Sikhism
1 God - oneness and equality
2 Living as a Sikh - Baisakhi and commitment

Prayer
Dear Jesus, open our hearts to accept all people.
Give us the strength we need to be kind with those who seem different from us.
Guide all that we think, do and say, as we learn to love everyone, just as you do. Amen

LEARNING OBJECTIVE: reflect on similarities between Christianity and other religions

Starting Points

We believe that God became man and walked with us. Jesus is God-and-man. Jesus gives us the full truth about God, and that is why it is not possible for Christians to agree with many things that other faiths believe.

There is an opportunity here to recall on the history of Salvation seeing a line of continuity between the story of Creation, Abraham, Moses, the prophets and that God sends his only Son, Jesus to show us the Way, to teach us the Truth and to give us new Life through the Sacraments.

Additional Activities
Worksheets 'Does it matter what you believe?' and 'What Christians believe' pages 83, 84.

In order to help pupils recall what they have learnt and make connections between the modules have a quiz: see the worksheet 'What We Believe & Why' page 85 This will give the children the opportunity to research the answers before hand and to work in teams of mixed ability so that the brighter pupils will help the weaker ones.

Worksheet 'What Christians Believe' page 84 is a chance for children to use the knowledge from the quiz and to tell their story, for example:
- God created us so that we can know, love and serve him here on earth and be happy with him forever.
- The freedom was misused.
- God sent great leaders to guide his people such as Moses who gave us the Ten Commandments.
- Eventually God sent his only Son, Jesus. Jesus is God-made-man. So in Jesus we know what God is like.

People of Other Faiths

ICT
www.bbc.co.uk/religion/religions/ Background information on the different religions for teachers
www.hitchams.suffolk.sch.uk/mosque/default.htm A school website on Islam
www.assemblies.org.uk/standing/world_religions/index.html Material for assemblies on different religions

Videos
BBC Pathways of Belief Judaism, Christianity, Islam, Hinduism & Sikhism

Index for Photocopy Worksheets

Gifts from God - Photocopy Worksheets
Stewards of the Earth 52
Humans / Animals 53
De-Creators 54
A Persuasive Letter! 55
Adam 56
Whose Fault Was It? 57
The World 58
Canticle of St Francis 59

The Commandments - Photocopy Worksheets
The Ten Commandments 60
Christmas 61

Inspirational People - Photocopy Worksheets
People I Admire 62
Love Your Enemies 63
A Saint Who Inspires Me 64
My Brother Michael 65
Profile of an Inspirational Person 67
Saints on the Web 68
Plans to Become an Inspirational Person 69

Reconciliation - Photocopy Worksheets
Consequences of My Actions 70
Gifts from God Sin Damages the Gifts 71
The Story of the Lost Son 72
My Conscience 73
Zachaeus 74
Stations of the Cross 75

Life in the Risen Jesus - Photocopy Worksheets
Prepare to Meet the Police! 76
The Latest News 77
Prayer Symbol 78
Prayers to help Us 79
The Mysteries of the Rosary 81
The Rosary 82

People of Other Faiths - Photocopy Worksheets
Does It Matter What You Believe? 83
What Christians Believe 84
What We Believe & Why 85

Photocopy Worksheets - Gifts from God

Stewards of the Earth

Two young people started to make a game called 'Stewards of the Earth'. With a partner make up the rest of the game or design your own.

Think about the rules and the equipment. Try to include these phrases and 5 more of your own;

- I take bottles to a bottle bank
- I throw litter on the ground
- I recycle cans
- I pick up litter in the playground

An excellent steward

Start

1.
2. I plant flowers. Go forward 1 space.
3.
4.
5.
6.
7.
8.
9.
10.
11.

Photocopy Worksheets - Gifts from God

Humans / Animals

In the spaces list all the things that we can do and that animals cannot do

Humans	Animals
Can...	Cannot...

53

De-Creators

Dear God,
Today, we want to reflect on the harmful things that are happening in the beautiful world you have given to us.

God made the atom
and we have made the atom bomb.

God made precious stones and metals,
and we have made weapons of destruction.

God made fire,
and we have burned our neighbour.

God made water,
and we have produced acid rain.

God made fresh air,
and we have invented pollution.

God made food in abundance,
and we have created starvation…

By Sr Leo OSC

Prayer

Dear God, for all these things we ask for your forgiveness:
Forgive us and forgive all the people who are doing harmful things to your creation. We ask you to enlighten all our minds so that we will understand and see the harmful effects of our actions.

Together let us pray 'Our Father…'
Choose a hymn or song to conclude

Photocopy Worksheets - Gifts from God

A Persuasive Letter!

How could you persuade someone who is a 'de-creator' to become a 'co-creator'?

Choose one of the following issues;
   Litter; Graffiti; River pollution; Rainforest; Waste.

I have chosen to write to .... about ....

Dear ....

Paragraph 1
Purpose of letter – I am writing because…

Paragraph 2
Explain what God has created for us.

Paragraph 3
Explain how this person's action is destroying God's world.

Paragraph 4
Suggest a way to improve the situation. What would happen if we changed?

With best wishes ....

Photocopy Worksheets - Gifts from God

Adam

*It wasn't me
it was that woman
she doesn't know what's good for her
she did it*

*and then
it was that snake
slimy horrible snake
I wouldn't have believed a word
I wouldn't have been taken in
imagine a talking snake
well I ask you*

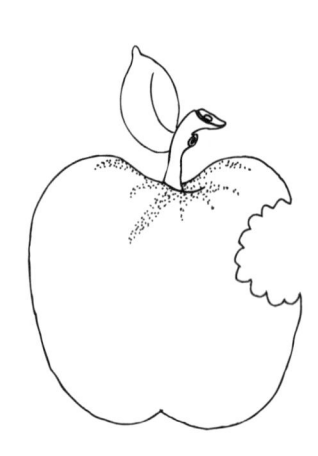

*and then
and then
it was you
you gave the serpent
it's your rotten apple
you knew all about it-
I was miles away
doing the garden like I was told
you're the one
you did it
it wasn't me
it wasn't me
and anyway I only took a little bite*

By G Rust

Activities

1. (a) Do you think Adam is telling the truth?
   (b) Give a reason why: Yes/No because ……………

2. Do you think Adam is responsible for what went wrong?
   Give a reason for your answer.

3. What would you want to say to Adam if you met him?

4. Do situations like this like ever happen today? If you think they do, describe one.

56

Photocopy Worksheets - Gifts from God

Whose Fault Was It?

The serpent asked the woman, 'did God really say you were not to eat from any of the trees in the garden?' The woman answered the serpent. 'We may eat the fruit of the trees in the garden. But of the fruit of the tree in the middle of the garden God said, "You must not eat it, nor touch it, under pain of death".' Then the serpent said to the woman, 'No! You will not die! God knows in fact that on the day you eat it your eyes will be opened and you will be like gods, knowing good and evil.' The woman saw that the tree was good to eat and pleasing to the eye, and that it was desirable for the knowledge that it could give. So she took some of its fruit and ate it. She gave some also to her husband who was with her, and he ate it. *(Gen. 3:1-7)*

Activities

Whose fault was it that Adam ate the fruit from the tree in the middle of the garden?

1. What do you think?

I think it was _____ *'s fault because* _____

2. Interview 5 pupils in the class to see what they think.
Use the chart below to compile their views.

PUPIL	SNAKE	ADAM	EVE	GOD
1.				
2.				
3.				
4.				
5.				

The majority of pupils think it was _____ *'s fault because* _____

A few pupils think it was _____ *'s because* _____

The World

Great, wide, beautiful, wonderful World.
With the wonderful water round you curled,
And the wonderful grass upon your breast –
World, you are beautifully dressed.

The wonderful air is over me,
And the wonderful wind is shaking the tree,
It walks on the water, and whirls the mills,
And talks to itself on the tops of the hills.

You friendly Earth, how far do you go,
With the wheat-fields that nod and the rivers that flow,
With cities and gardens, and cliffs, and isles,
And people upon you for thousands of miles?

Ah, you are so great, and I am so small,
I tremble to think of you, World, at all;
And yet, when I said my prayers today,
A whisper inside me seemed to say,
"You are more than the Earth, though you are such a dot;
You can love and think, and the Earth cannot".

By W Brighty Rands

Activity

Work in pairs
   (a) Try to find pictures on the Internet to illustrate this poem.
       Then make a display of picture and verse.

Or

   (b) Use this poem to make a Power Point presentation with pictures
       to use for Collective Worship in school.

Photocopy Worksheets - Gifts from God

Canticle of St Francis

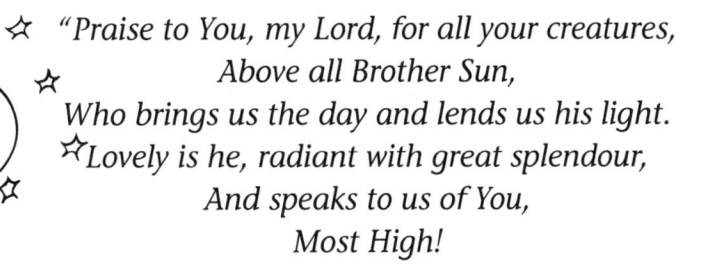

"Praise to You, my Lord, for all your creatures,
Above all Brother Sun,
Who brings us the day and lends us his light.
Lovely is he, radiant with great splendour,
And speaks to us of You,
Most High!

Praise to You, my Lord, for Sister Moon and all the stars,
Which You have set in the heavens,
Clear, precious and fair.

Praise to You, my Lord, for Brother Wind,
For air and cloud, for calm and all weather,
By which You support life in all your creatures.

Praise to You, my Lord, for Sister Water,
Who is so useful and humble,
Precious and pure.

Praise to You, my Lord, for Brother Fire,
By whom You light the night;
He is lovely and kind, mighty and strong.

Praise to You, my Lord, for our sister, Mother Earth,
Who comforts and looks after us,
And brings forth fruits, right-coloured flowers and herbs.

Praise and bless my Lord,
Thank Him and serve Him,
With all humility."

Leader	**Response**
For the sun moon and stars	We praise you, Lord
For the birds and animals	We praise you, Lord
For the trees and flowers	We praise you, Lord
For the rivers and mountains	We praise you, Lord
For our family and friends	We thank you, Lord
For teachers and all who help us	We thank you, Lord
For our work and play	We thank you, Lord
For another new day	We thank you, Lord

Photocopy Worksheets - The Commandments

The Ten Commandments

Activity

The Commandments have got mixed up.

Match them up by colouring in the parts that go together.
Or
Put numbers on them to show which one it is.

- I am the Lord your God
- Honour your father
- of your neighbour's belongings
- steal
- You shall not tell lies
- You shall not be envious of
- Remember to keep
- You shall not
- your neighbour's wife
- kill
- and your mother
- the Lord's Day holy
- You shall not commit
- You shall not use the name of the Lord
- You shall not
- You shall not be envious
- you shall have no other gods before me
- adultery
- about your neighbour
- wrongly

60

Christmas

A Thinking Christmas

A turkey dinner
at Christmas
is great!

> *THINK*
> Somewhere... a boy
> with an empty plate.

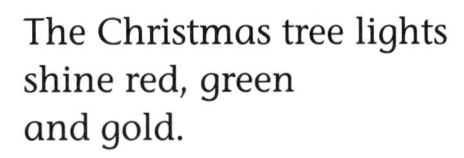

The Christmas tree lights
shine red, green
and gold.

> *THINK*
> Somewhere... a girl
> shivering and cold

Presents, and parties!
Yes, that's
Christmas Day!

> *THINK*
> Somewhere... a babe
> asleep in the hay.

By Wes Magee

A Joyful Christmas!

Think about how you could make it a Joyful Christmas.
Write your own poem as a reminder of how you can give pleasure to others at Christmas.
Think about what you have been studying this term and the most important things you can do to give pleasure to others.

Photocopy Worksheets - Inspirational People

People I Admire

In the middle of the star write the name of the person you admire.
Underneath the star say why you think that person inspires you.
On top of the star write the quality you admire most in that person.

Photocopy Worksheets - Inspirational People

Love Your Enemies
Luke 6:27-37

Love of enemies

"I say to this to you who are listening: Love your enemies, do good to those who hate you, bless those who curse you, pray for those who treat you badly.

To the man who slaps you on one cheek, present the other cheek too. To the man who takes your cloak from you, do not refuse your tunic. Give to everyone who asks you, and do not ask for your property back from the man who robs you. Treat others as you would like them to treat you.

If you love those who love you, what thanks can you expect? Even sinners love those who love them. And if you do good to those who do good to you, what thanks can you expect? For even sinners do that much. And if you lend to those from whom you hope to receive, what thanks can you expect? Even sinners lend to sinners to get back the same amount.

Instead, love your enemies and do good, and lend without any hope of return. You will have a great reward, and you will be sons of the Most High, for he himself is kind to the ungrateful and the wicked.

Compassion and generosity

"Be compassionate as your Father is compassionate. Do not judge, and you will not be judged yourselves; do not condemn and you will not be condemned yourselves; grant pardon, and you will be pardoned."

Activity

Use the words of Jesus to design a 'Membership Card' for those who want to be his close followers. You may also add other things he says about being a disciple, for example, Matthew 18:22.

A Saint Who Inspires Me

Saint .... inspires me because ....

I think .... will help other people because ....

....

Saint .... will be remembered forever because ....

....

I found my information about Saint .... on ....

I .... doing this work because ....

My brother Michael

Michael and I are twins and we are the youngest children in a family of six. We are great friends, although we have some really amazing rows!

On February 6th, Michael and I were competing at our local gymkhana. It was a big day and secretly we were keen to beat each other in the junior jumping class. I completed my round with only four faults and then Michael and I teased each other in the collecting ring before he went in for his turn. It was a great morning and I remember my father offering a £10 prize to the eventual victor!

The family cheered as Michael cleared the first few fences and then I vividly remember the sound of a vicious dogfight dominating the arena, followed by the piercing screams of my mother. Someone led me away and I recall ambulance sirens and loudspeaker announcements calling for a doctor.

For eight months Michael lay in his hospital bed, unable to move, attached to so many machines, it was unbelievable. The first time I saw him I could hardly bear to look at him, I couldn't believe this was my brother. Everyone spoke in low whispered tones and although I was continually told everything would be all right, I didn't believe them.

Michael underwent ten operations in the space of four months and numerous intensive physiotherapy sessions only to be told that he would never walk again.

My bitterness and anger was shared by so many members of our family but never by Michael. He simply wanted to get on with life. He pushed himself to the limit, amazing everyone with his guts and determination. I remember watching the end of one of his treatment routines in the pool. He came out crying with pain, but he had refused to give up. Mum cried, as she watched him punishing himself and I did not understand it at all – it made me feel sick.

All this happened three years ago and Michael is now at home and continuing his studies. Our house was converted to accommodate his wheelchair and he has numerous gadgets to help him cope with everyday life. He is determined to enjoy life and to use the gifts God has given to him. His latest ambition is to compete in driving competitions, once his pony has been trained to pull his carriage!

When I see him dragging his body out of his chair and into the carriage, it is easy to feel pity, but Michael has never wanted that, he only wants to get on with life, and he has taught me to do the same.

Activities

God has given each one of us many gifts or talents and invites us to use them to the best of our ability.

1. (a) In what way, do you think, Michael is using his gifts?

(b) What do you think is the most inspirational part of the story?

(c) If you could ask Michael a question about his experience what would it be? Why?

2. Think of all the people you know. Choose the one you believe makes the best use of his/her gifts and write a story about that person.

Profile of an Inspirational Person

Choose somebody who has inspired you and use the following to help you collect information about that person.

Name:

Country of origin:

Personal qualities:

Work:

What you admire in him/her:

What do you think has helped this person most in life:

Will other people remember this person?

Why or why not?

Photocopy Worksheets - Inspirational People

Saints on the Web

What is a saint?	*www.ainglkiss.com/saints/*
Do we worship saints?	*www.ainglkiss.com/saints/*
St Clare	*www.ainglkiss.com/saints/clare.htm*
St Rose of Lima	*www.ainglkiss.com/saints/rose.htm*
St Teresa of Avila	*www.ainglkiss.com/saints/thera.htm*
St Therese	*www.ainglkiss.com/saints.ther.htm*
St Dominic Savio	*www.ainglkiss.com/saints/sav.htm*
St Brigid of Ireland	*www.adena.com/adena/sts/brigid.htm*
St Nicholas	*www.cptryon.org/prayer/child/nick.html*
St Patrick	*www.ainglkiss.com/saints/pat.htm*
St Thomas More	*www.ainglkiss.com/saints/tmor.htm*
St Maria Goretti	*www.ainglkiss.com/saints/maria.htm*
St Philip Neri	*www.ainglkiss.com/saints/philner.htm*
St Lucy	*www.ainglkiss.com/saints/lucy.htm*
St Joan of Arc	*www.ainglkiss.com/saints/joa/htm*
St Gabriel of Our Lady of Sorrows	*www.ainglkiss.com/saints/gab.htm*
St Aloysius Gonzaga	*www.ainglkiss.com/saints/alo.htm*
St Anthony of Padua	*www.ainglkiss.com/saints.anth.htm*
St Vincent de Paul	*www.ainglkiss.com/saints/depa.htm*

Photocopy Worksheets - Inspirational People

Plans to Become an Inspirational Person

Think of 10 things you could do in the next 10 years to become an Inspirational person and write them in each box. The first is done for you.

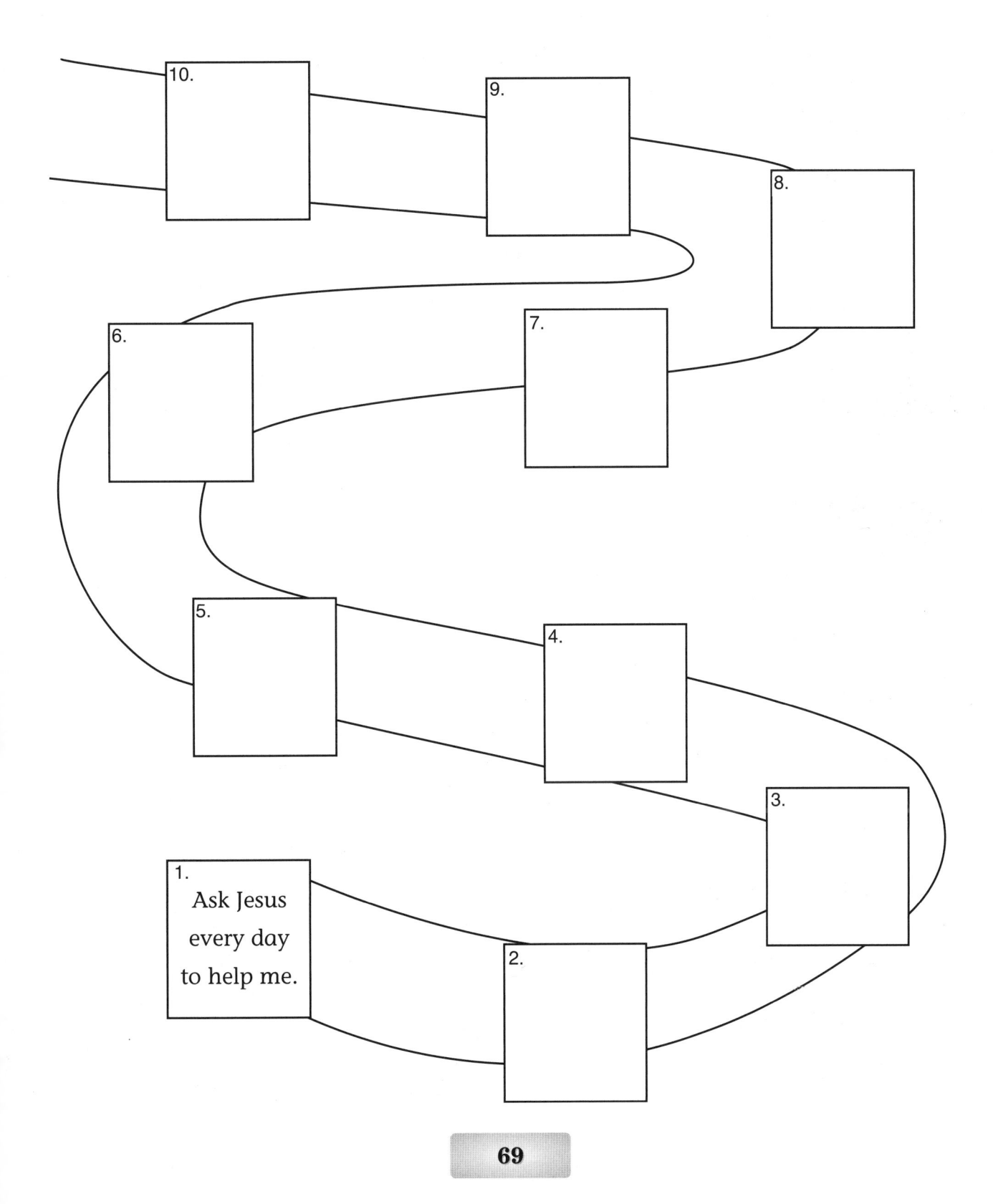

1. Ask Jesus every day to help me.

2.
3.
4.
5.
6.
7.
8.
9.
10.

69

Photocopy Worksheets - Reconciliation

Consequences of My Actions

1. In the circle write in different sections **ME, FAMILY, SCHOOL, OTHERS**
2. Choose a situation on pages 50 and 51 of your text book. Copy it onto the top of this sheet.
3. In each section of the circle explain how such behaviour would affect the people.

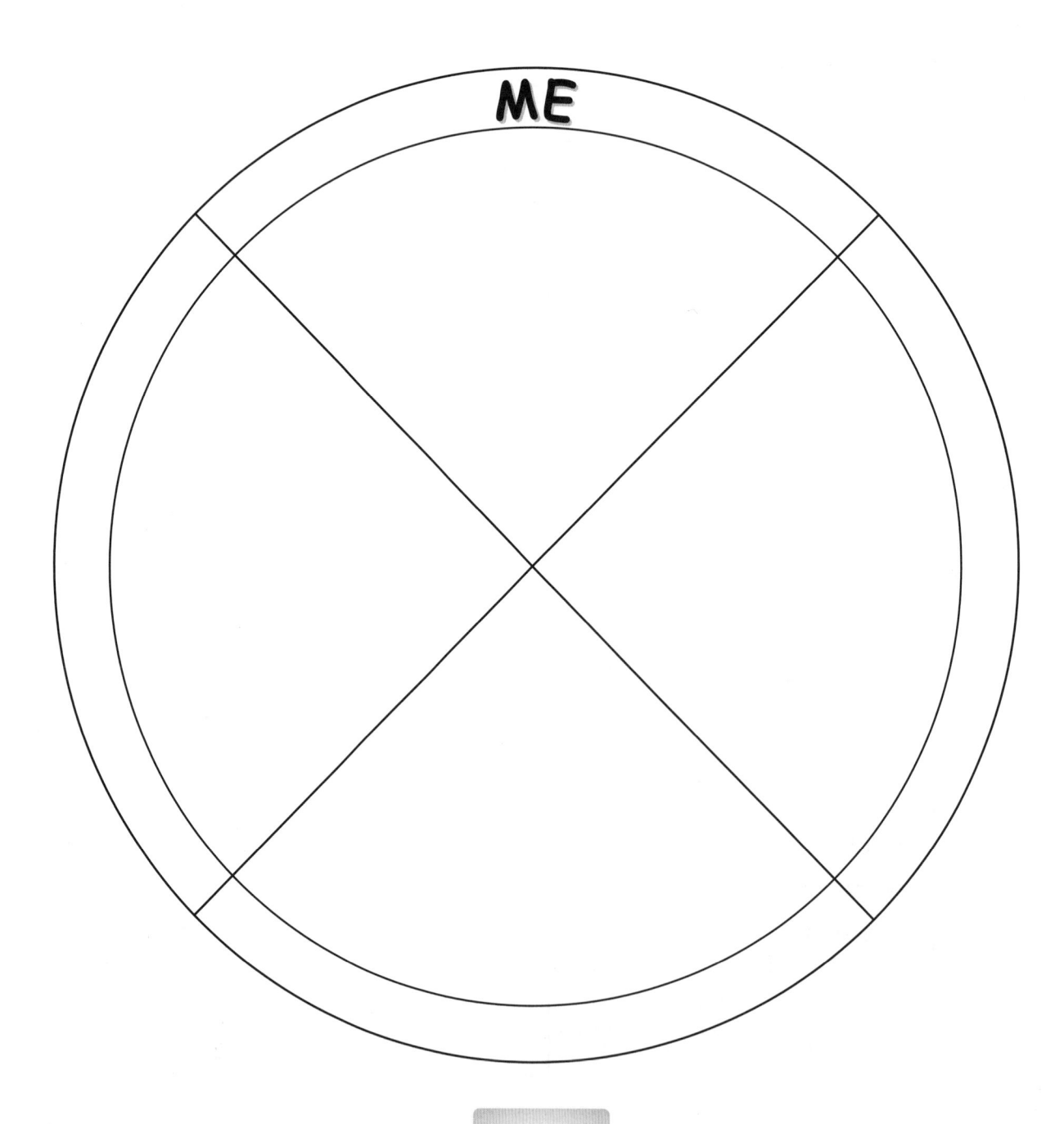

ME

Photocopy Worksheets - Reconciliation

Gifts from God
Sin Damages the Gifts

1. Select four gifts God has give to you from the box and put them in the top shapes.
2. Fill the other boxes with words which can damage these gifts.

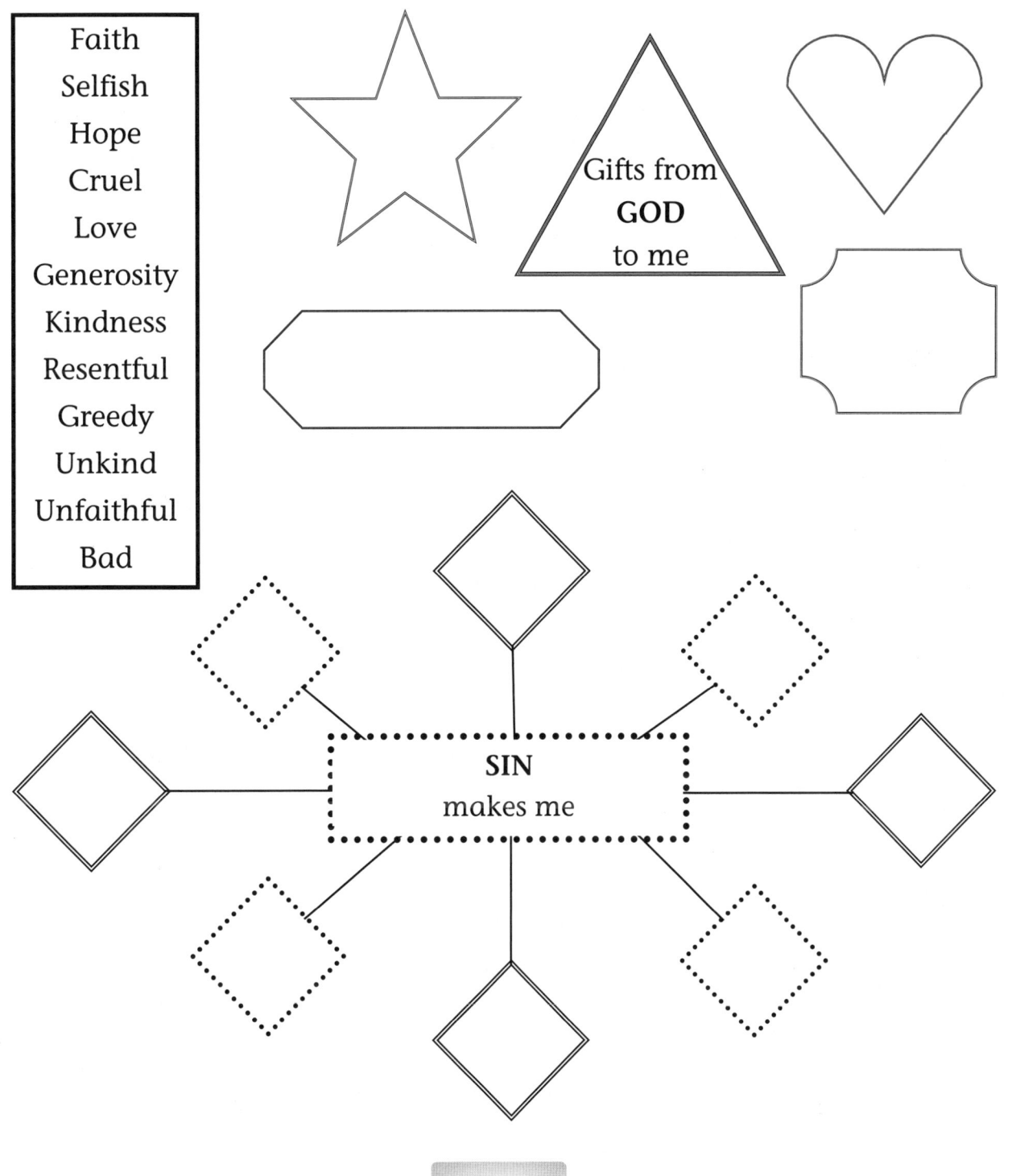

Faith
Selfish
Hope
Cruel
Love
Generosity
Kindness
Resentful
Greedy
Unkind
Unfaithful
Bad

Gifts from **GOD** to me

SIN makes me

Photocopy Worksheets - Reconciliation

The Story of the Lost Son

Complete the story by filling in the missing words from the word box.

Word Box
away
afraid
ring
left
younger
sons
money
lonely
hungry
father
servant
forgive
shoes
robe
dead
sinned
party
lost
brother
noise
jealous
brother
good
found
brother
celebrate
alive

A man has two _____. One day, the _____ son asked his father to give him his share of the inheritance. When he got it he _____ home. He went far _____ and lived a life of luxury and spent all his _____. Then a famine came and he was very _____. He got a job looking after pigs. He was very _____ and _____ so he thought to himself, "I will go back to my _____ and ask him to _____ me.

While he was still a long way off, his father saw him and said to his _____: "Bring the best _____ and clothe him. Give him a _____ for his finger, and _____ for his feet. When the son met his father he said "Father, I have _____ against you and against God. I should no longer be called your son". But the father said, "NO! I thought your were _____ but you are alive. You were _____ but now you are found. Let us have a big _____."

The elder brother, coming home from work, heard the _____. When he heard that his _____ had come back and there was going to be a big celebration, he was _____. He said to his father, "I have always been a _____ son and you did not reward me, but now my _____ has returned and you give him a party". The father answered him, "You are always here with me, and all if have is yours, but we have to _____ and be happy, because your _____ was dead and is now _____. He was lost and is _____."

Photocopy Worksheets - Reconciliation

My Conscience

When I am trying to decide if something is right or wrong I use my conscience. Conscience is that feeling inside that tells you what is right and what is wrong. It is like God's little bell.

I have a duty to inform my conscience so that I will make the right decisions. I inform my conscience by listening to the advice of those who have a responsibility for me, for example, my parents or teachers. I must also listen to Jesus and what the Church teaches.

These are the ways in which I must form my conscience so that it does not lead me away from the truth. Each day I must ask Jesus to help me make the right decisions.

Activities

1. In your own words explain:
Conscience is ....

....

2. To inform my conscience I need to ....

....

3. I use my conscience when I ....

....

4. Use this website www.ainglkiss.com/xam/4kids/ to make notes to help you with an Examination of Conscience.

Photocopy Worksheets - Reconciliation

Zachaeus

In the Gospels we are told that Jesus healed many people of their sins, restoring their friendship with God and one another.

Zachaeus was someone who was changed through a personal meeting with Jesus, which enabled him to make a fresh start and heal some of the broken personal relationships he had caused.

Activities

1. Read the opening of Zachaeus's letter to a friend. Copy it into your book and complete it.

> Dear Nathan,
>
> Today my life was changed because of a truly amazing meeting with Jesus of Nazareth. Much to my surprise He stopped under the sycamore tree, where I had perched myself in order to get a close look at this man they are all talking about, and He asked to come to my place for tea. Thankfully I had swept the floors that very morning! Anyway, we chatted over a glass of wine and Jesus said,

2. **(a)** What do you think was the most important moment in the story of Zachaeus?

   (b) Explain what was important about that moment.

   (c) Imagine what this event looked like, sketch it on half a page in your book and write a caption for it.

Photocopy Worksheets - Reconciliation

Stations of the Cross

Write a caption for each of the Stations of the Cross in the box beside the picture.

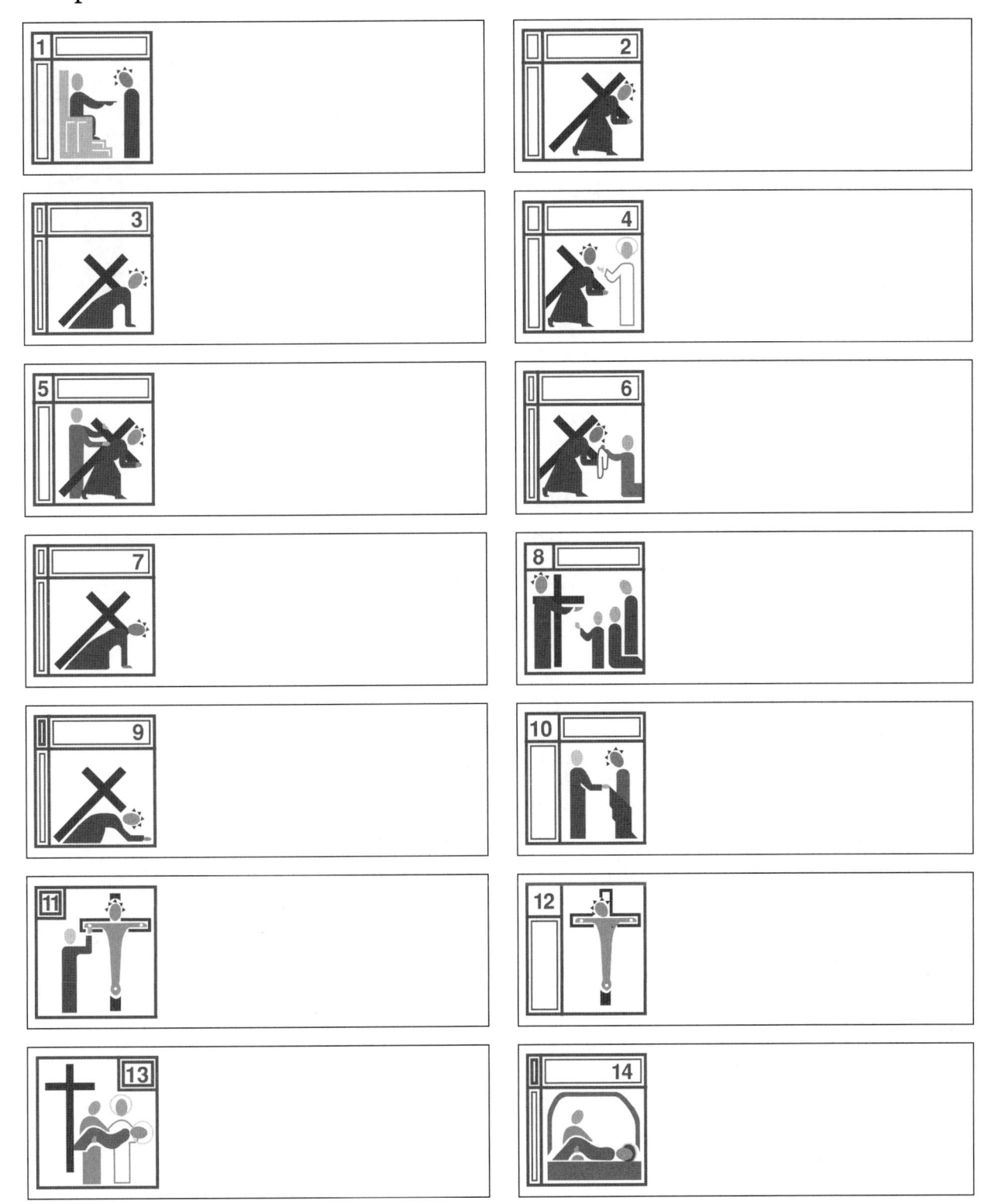

75

Prepare to Meet the Police!

What to do:

1. Read the account of the appearance of Jesus; remember you must imagine that you are an eyewitness in this story.

2. Read the story a second time. Highlight or copy out the following points.

    (a) What did Jesus say?

    (b) Where did you meet Jesus?

    (c) How do you know it was Jesus and not a ghost?

3. Did Jesus ever tell you he was going to rise from the dead? This is a difficult question and you might want to say 'No' or you may want to do some **research**, for example in St John's Gospel look up the following references: 11:25 or 14:18 or 16:16.

4. If you are asked 'What do you think is going to happen now?'

    (a) Think about how seeing Jesus alive has helped you to believe that he is truly the Saviour who will give us eternal life.

    (b) Think about how other people will come to believe in Jesus.

    (c) Think about how everyone will try to put the teaching of Jesus into practice and the world will be a better place to live in.

    (d) Do you know anything about who Jesus will send to help us?

    (e) Can you think of anything else? Make notes on all these points to help you remember.

Photocopy Worksheets - Life in the Risen Jesus

The Latest News

1. Study the front page of a newspaper; note how the headlines are set out and how the important facts stand out.

2. Imagine you are a journalist writing about the resurrection of Jesus.

3. You can use this sheet or design your own. If you use this one, put the headline in box 1, put a picture in box 2, give a short summary of the most important facts in box 3 and write your account in boxes 4 and 5.

4. Points to consider:
    Say what happened on Good Friday.
    When did the news come out that Jesus was alive?
    Who saw him?
    Did he speak to anyone? What did he say?
    Has anyone else seen him?
    Why do you think this news is very important?

Photocopy Worksheets - Life in the Risen Jesus

Prayers to help Us

Morning Offering

Dear Jesus, I offer you my work, my happiness and my fears today.
Please take care of my family, my friends, and me.
Mary, dearest Mother, help me to grow like Jesus in everything I do.

Night Prayer

Dear Jesus, before I sleep tonight,
I want to thank you for being with me today.
As I go to bed, keep me and all those dear to me
in your loving care.

The Angelus

The Angel of the Lord declared unto Mary
And she conceived of the Holy Spirit.
Hail Mary…

Behold the handmaid of the Lord.
Be it done unto me according to thy word.
Hail Mary…

And the Word was made flesh
And dwelt among us
Hail Mary…

Pray for us, O holy Mother of God,
that we may be made worthy of the promises of Christ.

Let us pray
Pour forth we beseech you, O Lord, thy grace into our hearts; that we to whom the incarnation of Christ your Son was made known by the message of an angel, may, by his passion and cross be brought to the glory of his resurrection. Through Christ, Our Lord, Amen.

Photocopy Worksheets - Life in the Risen Jesus

Prayer to the Holy Spirit

Come, Holy Spirit, fill the hearts of your faithful
and kindle in them the fire of your love.
Send forth your Spirit and there will be a new creation
and you will renew the face of the earth.

Let us pray:
O God, you instruct the hearts of the faithful by the light of the Holy Spirit, grant that by the same Holy Spirit we may choose what is right and ever rejoice in his consolation, through Christ, Our Lord, Amen.

Prayer to the Guardian Angel

Angel of God, my guardian dear,
to whom God's love commits me here,
ever this day be at my side
to light and guard, to rule and guide. Amen.

Grace before Meals

Bless us, O Lord, and these thy gifts,
Which we are about to receive from thy bounty,
through Christ, Our Lord, Amen.

Grace after Meals

We give you thanks, almighty God, for all these gifts
which we have received from your goodness,
through Christ, Our Lord, Amen.

The Memorare

Remember, O most loving Virgin Mary, that it is a thing unheard of,
that anyone ever had recourse to your protection, implored your help,
or sought your intercession, and was left forsaken.
Filled, therefore, with confidence in your goodness
I fly to you, O Mother, Virgin of virgins.
To you I come, before you I stand, a sorrowful sinner.
Despise not my poor words, O Mother of the Word of God,
but graciously hear and grant my prayer. Amen.

Website: Try *www.cptryon.org/prayer/child/index.html*
You will find: Sign of the Cross; Our Father; Glory to the Father; Hail Mary; The Apostles Creed, a collection of everyday prayers and explainations of prayers.

The Mysteries of the Rosary

The Joyful Mysteries
The Annunciation
The Visitation
The Nativity
The Presentation
The Finding in the Temple

The Mysteries of Light
The Baptism in the Jordan
The Wedding at Cana
The Proclamation of the Kingdom
The Transfiguration
The Institution of the Eucharist

The Sorrowful Mysteries
The Agony in the Garden
The Scourging at the Pillar
The Crowning with Thorns
The Carrying of the Cross
The Crucifixion

The Glorious Mysteries
The Resurrection
The Ascension
The Descent of the Holy Spirit
The Assumption
The Crowning of our Lady in Heaven, and the Glory of all the Saints

Photocopy Worksheets - Life in the Risen Jesus

The Rosary

The meanings of the Mysteries of the Rosary have got mixed up.
(a) Choose one set of Mysteries
(b) Put the explanation with each one and your own illustration.
(c) Choose one mystery in the set you have chosen and tell the story of it.

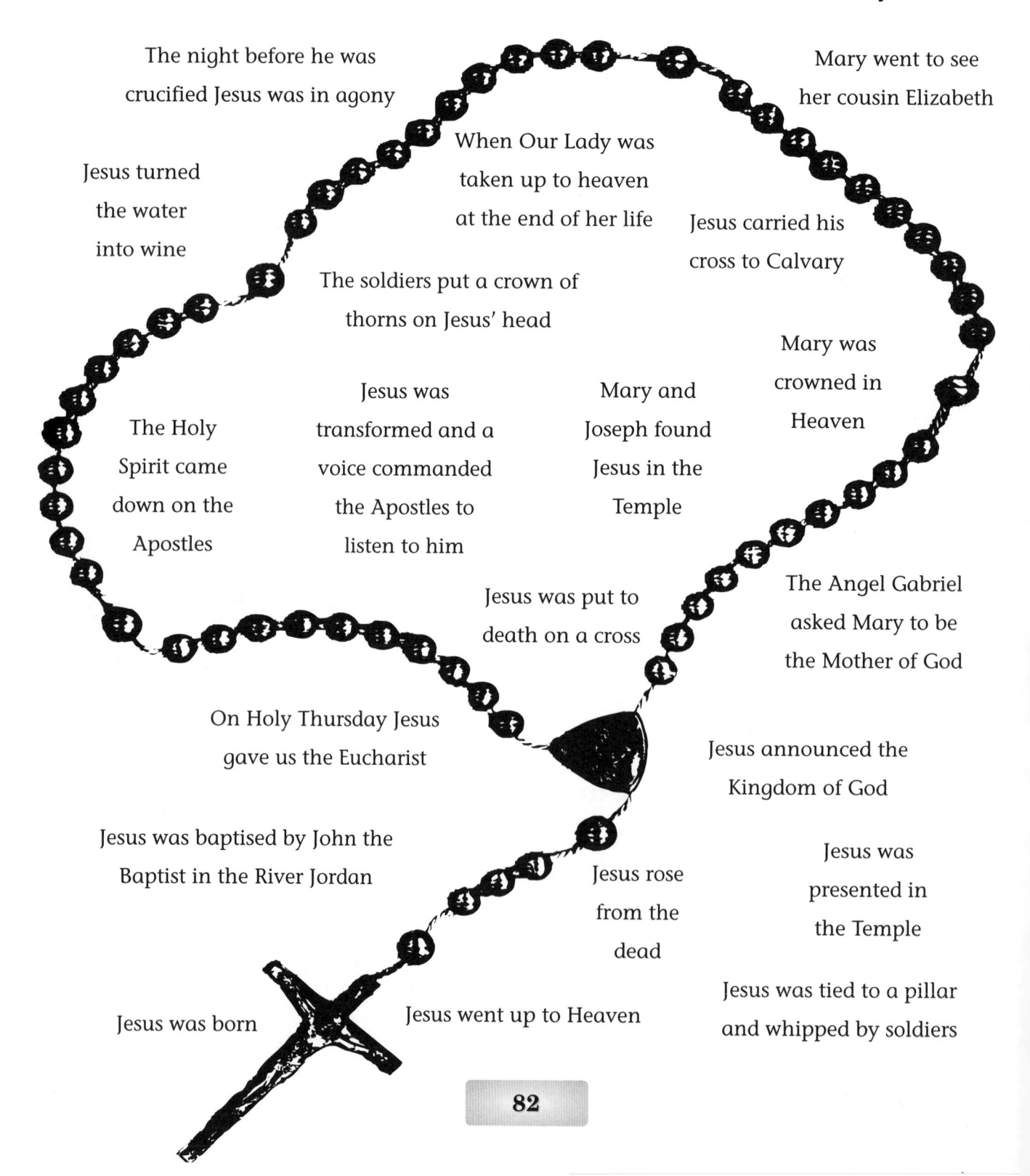

The night before he was crucified Jesus was in agony

Mary went to see her cousin Elizabeth

Jesus turned the water into wine

When Our Lady was taken up to heaven at the end of her life

Jesus carried his cross to Calvary

The soldiers put a crown of thorns on Jesus' head

Mary was crowned in Heaven

The Holy Spirit came down on the Apostles

Jesus was transformed and a voice commanded the Apostles to listen to him

Mary and Joseph found Jesus in the Temple

Jesus was put to death on a cross

The Angel Gabriel asked Mary to be the Mother of God

On Holy Thursday Jesus gave us the Eucharist

Jesus announced the Kingdom of God

Jesus was baptised by John the Baptist in the River Jordan

Jesus rose from the dead

Jesus was presented in the Temple

Jesus was born

Jesus went up to Heaven

Jesus was tied to a pillar and whipped by soldiers

Photocopy Worksheets - People of Other Faiths

Does It Matter What You Believe?

Listen as the story of the Prince and the Elephant is being read.

The story of the Prince and the Elephant (part 1)

An Eastern Prince was tired out by the arguments among his advisors. They quarrelled about what God was really like. So he arranged for an animal, a rare animal, an animal that no one in the country had ever seen, to be brought into a large room in his palace. He then gathered his advisors into the room next door. The Prince challenged each advisor to tell him what kind of creature was in the next room. As a catch, he made them enter the room blindfolded, and touch only that part of the creature they came to first. The first advisor touched the elephant's long trunk, the second advisor a flapping ear, the third advisor the great belly of the elephant. On returning to the prince each advisor was asked to say what kind of creature the Prince had in the next room.

'It is, O Prince, a giant snake. A snake with wrinkles.' said the first advisor (who had touched the trunk).

'Nonsense,' said the second advisor (who had touched the ear), 'it is, O Prince, a giant flying creature with leather wings.'

'You're both wrong,' said the third advisor (who had touched the belly), 'it is, O Prince, a giant living rock.'

The Prince declared that they were all wrong. They could only describe a little part of the creature as being the whole of it. The same is true of God, the Prince went on, because we don't really know what God is like since we cannot see him.

1. Do you agree or disagree with the Prince? Say why.

2. What do you think the message of the story is?

83

What Christians Believe

Christians would not accept the message of the story of the Prince and the Elephant (Part 1). They believe that there should be other parts to it. Part 2 of the story would go like this:

The story of the Prince and the Elephant (part 2)

But no sooner had the Prince stopped speaking when the elephant stepped out of the room for all to see. One by one, all the advisors, all the courtiers and everyone else gathered got to see the elephant for what it truly was.

The advisors realised how wrong they had been. Their vague ideas about what kind of creature the elephant was had vanished. Now, with the elephant waving his trunk before them, they had a much better and clearer idea.

One of the advisors had the courage to speak up: 'Perhaps, O Prince, if God were to show himself clearly, we would all begin to know and understand God more fully.'

'Perhaps,' the Prince replied, thinking very deeply.

Activities

1. Work in pairs. Draw up a plan to write Part 3 of the story, which explains to the Prince and his advisors that God has come among us and we know what he is like.

Or

2. Write a letter to the Prince. Tell him how you know about God and where you find your information.

Photocopy Worksheets - People of Other Faiths

What We Believe & Why

Quiz
- Work in Teams
- Here are the questions, so that you can prepare your answers.
- The number in brackets after each question refers to pages in Book 5 – this will provide a clue of where to find the answers to the questions.
- You can make notes, but you have to put them away when the quiz starts.

Questions

1. Who created the world? (4)

2. Why did God make us? (5)

3. What are the names of the first man and woman in the Bible? (12)

4. Why did they lose their special friendship with God? (13)

5. If God made the world why is there suffering in it? (12)

6. What is the first sin called? (14)

7. Does that sin affect us? (14)

8. Name two of the great leaders God chose to guide his people. (20)

9. What did God give to Moses for the people? (21)

10. Give one reason why God sent his Son, Jesus, into the world. (A bonus point for a second reason.) (32)

11. Give two examples of what it means to be a follower of Jesus. (A bonus point for a third example.) (34, 38)

12. What will happen if we do something that offends God? (52)

13. What does Jesus teach us about forgiveness?n (58)

14. What happened to Jesus on Good Friday? (58)

15. What happened to Jesus on Easter Sunday? (64)

16. Mention two ways in which Jesus is present with us. (A bonus point for a third.) (68)

17. After the Resurrection, what did Jesus say to Thomas that will help us today? (John 20:19-29)

18. What does the Resurrection mean for us?

19. What does it mean to say that Jesus is the unique revelation of God? (90)

20. If we lead a good life and put the teaching of Jesus into practice what will happen when we die?

Levels of Achievement

ASSESSMENT & LEVELS OF ACHIEVEMENT

Introduction
Good assessment should have variety, flexibility and be based on the professional judgement of teachers. Schools will wish to develop a range of assessment tasks, such as spoken, creative or written work. Assessment should be on going, not added on.

Formative assessment
Formative assessment goes on all the time. It includes oral responses, self-evaluation, target setting, marking and Records of Achievement. It is formative because it points out what is good and how it could be improved.

Summative assessment
This summarises and reports on what has been learnt. It is helpful to create 'contexts' when setting tasks. One way of doing it is to create an imaginary problem. For example, Jessica has been away for two weeks. She has missed out on preparation for the Sacrament of Reconciliation. Can you tell her how to prepare, what happens when you go to Confession and what you do immediately afterwards?

Creation of the World: Two important things I've found out so far about Creation are;
1. _____
2. _____
I need help with _____
I enjoy _____

Before Confession: I need to do two things
1. _____
2. _____

At Confession:
1. Then I tell him what I have _____
2. The priest will give _____
3. I tell God that _____
4. God forgives _____
5. I say 'thank you' to _____

After Confession:
1. I thank God for _____

Self evaluation
The following prompts may help pupils to assess their own learning.

Inspirational People
I wrote about _____ because _____

What I admire most about _____ is the way _____ because _____

I think other people should know about _____ because _____

I enjoyed doing this work because _____

I can improve by _____

Levels of Achievement

The following is guidance for teachers to help them map pupils' progress. Teachers may feel that they also need to give pupils feedback in a different form in order to motivate and give them a sense of achievement.

The Level Descriptors are based on National Expectations in Religious Education produced by the Qualifications and Curriculum Authority (QCA). The QCA descriptors have been modified so that they apply specifically to Catholic religious education content.

The overview on page 88 provides examples of how a pupil might attain a particular level. The exemplar assessment tasks based on each module or unit of work are intended as guidance for the teacher.

Attainment Target 1 (AT1) = Learning **ABOUT** the Catholic Faith

Attainment Target 2 (AT2) = Learning **FROM** the Catholic Faith

OVERVIEW of GRID
A B C = AT1
D E F = AT2

Range of levels within which the majority of pupils are expected to work	Expected attainment for the majority of pupils at the end of the key stage
Key Stage 1 L1 - 3	At the age of 7 L2
Key Stage 2 L2 - 5	At the age of 11 L4

Levels of Achievement

Level	A **Beliefs & teachings** (what people believe)	B **Practices & lifestyles** (what people do)	C *Expression & language* *(how people express themselves)*	D *Identity & experience* *(making sense of who we are)*	E *Meaning & purpose* *(making sense of life)*	F *Values & commitments* *(making sense of right & wrong)*
1	Tell a story	Recognise what we are doing when e.g. we pray	Recognise the meaning of some words: e.g. Holy Communion; Sacrament of Reconciliation	Be able to say why it is important to learn about e.g. Jesus, forgiveness	Realise that some questions that cause people to wonder are difficult to answer	Know the difference between a good action and a bad one
2	Indicate what is important about it	What are some of the things Christians do? Do other religions do these things?	Suggest their meaning	Respond sensitively to the feelings of others	Be aware that some questions are difficult to answer, e.g. Who is God?	Be sensitive to what people believe about matters of right & wrong
3	Describe a belief or teaching and say why it is important	What are some of the big events Christians celebrate? For example: Christmas, Easter	Explain the use of some religious language: e.g. Jesus died to take away our sins; to give us eternal life in heaven		Compare their own & other people's ideas about questions that are difficult to answer e.g. Why did Jesus die on the cross?	Make links between matters of right and wrong & their own behaviour
4	Describe the key beliefs and teaching of the religions studied and make some comparisons between religions	Show some understanding of what Catholics/Christians believe and how this should affect the way they live	Show how religious ideas & beliefs can be expressed in a variety of forms, giving meanings for some parables or prayers of the Church	Ask questions about key figures & suggest answers from own and other's experience	Ask questions about significant experiences of key figures and suggest answers, e.g. What does the resurrection of Jesus mean for us?	Ask questions on matters of right & wrong; suggest answers that show understanding of moral & religious issues
5	Explain how some beliefs & teachings are shared by different religions and how they can make a difference to peoples' lives	Explain how the teaching of Jesus could make a difference to the lives of others: e.g. to love one another & to love your enemies (Jn 15:12 & Matt 5:44)		Make informed responses to questions of identity & experience in light of learning	Make informed responses to questions of meaning in light of learning, e.g. What is the message of some of the parables for us?	Make informed responses to moral issues in the light of learning, e.g. stealing, telling lies etc.